2001–2002 Annual Supplement to

THE PIANO BOOK

BUYING & OWNING A NEW OR USED PIANO

LARRY FINE

BROOKSIDE PRESS • BOSTON, MASSACHUSETTS

Brookside Press
P.O. Box 178, Jamaica Plain, Massachusetts 02130
(617) 522-7182
(800) 888-4741 (orders: Independent Publishers Group)

info@pianobook.com
www.pianobook.com

Printed in the United States of America

Distributed to the book trade by Independent Publishers Group,
814 North Franklin St., Chicago, IL 60610
(800) 888-4741 or (312) 337-0747

ISBN 1-929145-06-3 (print edition)
ISBN 1-929145-07-1 (electronic edition)

NOTICE

Reasonable efforts have been made to secure accurate information for this publication. Due in part to the fact that manufacturers and distributors will not always willingly make this information available, however, some indirect sources have been relied upon.

Neither the author nor publisher make any guarantees with respect to the accuracy of the information contained herein and will not be liable for damages—incidental, consequential, or otherwise—resulting from the use of the information.

INTRODUCTION

Given the long time span between new editions of *The Piano Book,* it's impractical to provide in the book itself the detailed model and price data that piano shoppers increasingly seek. Similarly, updated information about manufacturers and products is needed in a timely manner. This *Annual Supplement to The Piano Book,* published each August, is designed to fill that information gap. I hope this modest companion volume will effectively extend the "shelf life" of *The Piano Book* as a valuable reference work, and serve as an additional information resource for piano buyers and piano lovers.

Larry Fine

June, 2001

CONTENTS

MANUFACTURER and PRODUCT UPDATE

This section describes changes to companies, products, and brand names since the fourth edition of *The Piano Book* went to press in the Fall of 2000. If a company or brand name is not listed here, it means that there is nothing new of substance to report.

It is not intended, of course, that the information in this update section take the place of the reviews in *The Piano Book*. With some exceptions, the update is limited to changes of a factual nature only, whereas the main book contains, in addition, critical reviews, ratings, and recommendations. Readers should understand that, in most cases, changes in the quality of any particular brand of piano occur very slowly, over a period of many years, if at all. Only where there has been an abrupt change in company ownership, or a period of rapid technological or economic change in the country of origin, is there likely to be a change in quality worth worrying about. For that reason, the reviews in *The Piano Book* can still be considered reliable unless otherwise noted here.

ALTENBURG

Correction to web site address: www.altenburgpiano.com

ASTIN-WEIGHT

Correction to web site address: astin-weightpianos.uswestdex.com

BACHENDORFF (new listing)

Keyboard Distributors Inc.
2512 Palm Ridge
Las Vegas, Nevada 89134

866-469-2224
bachendorffpianos@hotmail.com
www.bachendorffpianos.com

Pianos made by: Daewoo, Kyungki-do, South Korea

These are the Korean-made Ibach pianos described under "Ibach" in *The Piano Book*. They are now being distributed in the U.S. under the Bachendorff name.

With regard to particular model designations, the "RC" models have Renner actions and, for the most part, traditional styling. The letter "S" at the end of the model indicates a straight leg, "A" a curved leg. Models beginning with "C" are decorator-style models without Renner actions. Models 115SE and 115AE are styled like the RC models, but without Renner actions. A Renner action can be added for an additional $1,200.

BALDWIN

including Chickering

The model E-100 console has been discontinued and replaced by two Eurostyle studios, 44" model E-101 in continental style without legs and 45" model E-102 in classic styling with legs and toeblocks. The model E260 Hamilton studio in polyester and with a Eurostyle folding fallboard replaces the model E250 with a sliding fallboard. All Eurostyle models now come with a cable-operated mute rail.

In the grands, the new model 225E is the model M (5' 2") in French Provincial styling. The 7' model SF-10 has been renamed SF-10E in honor of its adoption of the enhanced features of the upgraded Artist series grands (see *The Piano Book* for details).

The Chickering grands reported on in *The Piano Book* have been withdrawn and replaced by three new pianos—5' 4", 5' 9", and 6' 2"—in fourteen different models in five furniture styles. The plates and cabinets include some features taken from old Chickering designs. These models are the latest in a long series of joint ventures between Baldwin and Samick, and are made in the Samick factories in Korea. In my estimation, the quality should be much better than the Chickerings being withdrawn, probably comparable to other Samick-made instruments.

At the time of this writing, a new management team has just been installed at Baldwin. More product changes can be expected, but decisions had not been made at press time. [As this book goes to press, Baldwin has just announced its intent to reorganize under Chapter 11 of the U.S. Bankruptcy Code.]

BECHSTEIN, C.

Web site address: www.bechstein.de

The model D-280 concert grand has been redesigned, with a capo bar and duplex scale in the treble for better tonal projection. These features have also been added to the model A-189.

Bechstein has introduced a new series of very beautiful designer verticals called "ProBechstein" in 45½", 46½", and 49" sizes. In the pricing guide section, they are the models called "Balance," "Advance," and "Ars Nova."

BECKER, J.

All J. Becker verticals now feature agraffes throughout the scale. Model numbers followed by "CZ" use Czech Detoa actions.

BERGMANN

See "Young Chang"

BLÜTHNER

In honor of the company's 150th anniversary, Blüthner has introduced a Jubilee model which has a commemorative cast-iron plate in the style of the special-edition pianos of a century ago. Any grand piano model can be special-ordered with this commemorative plate.

In what is perhaps a world's "first," Blüthner has designed and built a piano for left-handed pianists. This is a completely "backwards" piano, with the treble keys, hammers, and strings on the left and the bass on the right. When it was introduced, a pianist gave a concert on it after only a couple of hours of practice! It is currently available in the 6' 10" and 9' 2" sizes.

BÖSENDORFER

Bösendorfer has introduced a new 9' 2" (model 280) concert grand. This model is in addition to the two other concert grands (9' and 9' 6") the company already produces. Unlike the others, however, which have 92 and 97 keys, respectively, this new model has only 88 keys. It also features a new scale design with a front duplex and new action geometry. The company says the new model is intended for concert pianists who would otherwise be distracted or intimidated by the presence of additional keys in the bass. To my ears, the new piano has better sustain in the treble than I usually find in Bösendorfer pianos, but otherwise has a characteristic Bösendorfer sound and feel.

BOSTON

The 49" vertical model UP-125 is being replaced with a completely redesigned 50" model UP-126. In the redesign, the wooden back has been made much heftier and the plate much more rigid to better resist torsional and bending stresses. The bass scale has been reworked with reduced string tension for smoother bass tone, and the soundboard taper and rib placement have been refined for better treble tone. Lastly, the music desk for the European-style case design has been improved so that it holds music more securely. Similar changes for the 52" model are scheduled for next year.

THE BRITISH PIANO MANUFACTURING COMPANY LTD. (new listing)

The British Piano Manufacturing Co. Ltd.
Woodchester Mills
Woodchester, Stroud,
Glos. GL5 5NW England

(44) 1453-872871
www.pianoforte.co.uk

This is the new name, address, and phone number for the company formerly known as Whelpdale, Maxwell & Codd. This company produces Welmar, Knight, Broadwood, Bentley, and now Woodchester pianos. It purchased Woodchester last year and moved the manufacturing facilities for all its brands to the Woodchester factory, formerly the Bentley factory (see *The Piano Book* for history). However, the U.S. contact for Woodchester (only) remains unchanged (see *The Piano Book* under "Woodchester").

CHICKERING

See "Baldwin"

DISKLAVIER

See "Yamaha"

ESSEX

Steinway, through its Boston Piano Co. subsidiary, introduced several "Essex" models in early 2001. These are manufactured in Korea by Young Chang. They include 5' 3" and 6' grands and 42" and 44" verticals. The two vertical models are of identical scale design, but the smaller one is in a continental-style cabinet. Some of the vertical cabinets look backward to styles of past decades of the twentieth century. The company says that a 48" vertical will be introduced in 2002. The grands are in Art Deco style. At press time, only the polished ebony version of the 6' grand had been announced. It is expected, however, that this model will be available in the same finishes as the 5' 3" model.

Steinway says that it designed these pianos using state-of-the-art structural analysis software similar to that used in the auto and aircraft industries, allowing it to test the effects of a large number of variables in a short amount of time without having to build innumerable prototypes. Like Boston pianos, the Essex line was designed with a lower tension duplex scale and a larger, tapered solid spruce soundboard, for potentially better sustain. The grands utilize rosette-shaped flanges for better action stability.

FAZIOLI

Corrections to review: Three lids are optional on the 10' 2" grand. The 5' 2" and 6' models utilize a Delignit pinblock as mentioned, but the larger models have Bolduc (Canadian) pinblocks. The Fazioli warranty has been increased to ten years.

Additional web site address: www.fazioli.com

FEURICH

U.S. contact:

Warfield Piano
821 Kent Avenue
Baltimore, Maryland 21228

410-747-7700
www.feurich.com

Pianos made by: Feurich Klavier-u.Flügelfabrikation GmbH, Gunzenhausen, Germany

This venerable German manufacturer is once again making pianos in its own factory. The models being offered at this time are 46½" (F118) and 48½" (F123) verticals and 5' 8" (F172) and 7' 5" (F227) grands. A 45½" model F116 is the same as the F118, but without casters, and model F117 is the same as the F118, but in a simpler cabinet.

FÖRSTER, AUGUST

New web site address: www.august-foerster.de

HOFMANN & SCHOLZ

This company says it now has its own key-making facilities.

IBACH

The Ibach-Daewoo joint venture mentioned in *The Piano Book* was sold by Daewoo to a music industry investment group called Veloce Ltd. The Korean-made pianos are being distributed in the U.S. under the name Bachendorff and in Canada under the name Royale. See "Bachendorff" for more information about the U.S.-distributed pianos.

IRMLER

Chinese-made Irmlers have been discontinued for the time being.

KAWAI

Additional web site address: www.shigerukawai.com

True to its reputation, Kawai has made even more changes to its product line. The model 505 and 605 furniture-style consoles have been discontinued and replaced with several 44½" models utilizing the same scale design as the 605. Model 506S is this piano in a simple, Indonesian-made studio-style cabinet. Although called a "studio" because of the cabinet style, it has a compressed action characteristic of a console. Model 606 is this piano in a furniture-style console and comes in two levels of cabinetry, the more expensive ones having inlayed veneers. Model CX-10 is the 506S in a Japanese-style, polyester-finished cabinet. It replaces the popular model CX-5H as Kawai's low-priced "studio." The 46½" furniture-style studio model 902 has been changed to model 906, with a stiffer back structure, all ABS action parts, and new cabinetry. Model K-25 is like the 48" model K-30, except in a simpler cabinet.

In the grands, the 5' model GM-2A has become model GM-10. The 5' 1" model GE-1A has been replaced by the GE-20, which has the features of the former GE-1AS model. A new 5' 5" model GE-30 has been introduced. It has the same scale as the model RX-1, but is like the other GE models structurally and in terms of its features (see *The Piano Book* for details on the differences between the RX, GE, and GM models). The Shigeru Kawai pianos are now available in five different models from 5' 10" to 7' 6".

KEMBLE

New address for U.S. distributor:

Kemble & Company Ltd.
577B Hackman Road
Lititz, Pennsylvania 17543

The "Cambridge" models have been discontinued. A new 46½" "Windsor" model has been added. This model has a fancier cabinet and a more powerful bass than the 45" "Traditional" model. The 52" vertical, formerly available only as a limited-edition designer model, is now available as a regular model.

KINGSBURG

Correction to web site address: www.kingsburgpiano.com

KNABE, WM.

The Knabe piano line made by Young Chang for PianoDisc has been discontinued, and the name has been sold to Samick. Plans are under development by Samick to make a new premium-level piano with the Knabe name.

MASON & HAMLIN

Mason & Hamlin is working on a new 6' 3" model AA grand, to be introduced in 2002 or 2003.

PEARL RIVER

New address and phone number for U.S. distributor:

Pearl River Piano Group America, Ltd.
1521 South Carlos Avenue
Ontario, California 91761

909-673-9155
800-435-5086
www.pearlriverpianos.com

Pearl River has added a 6' 4" grand to its regular line and a 49" vertical model 126R to its Ritmüller line. The vertical is based on the model 125M1 joint venture piano, but with agraffes throughout the scale.

Correction: The 4' 7" Ritmüller grand does not have a Renner action.

PETROF

Web site address: www.petrof.com

In Fall 2001, Petrof plans to introduce a new concert grand called the "P1 Mistral." The company says the instrument will use a more rigid brace and frame, front and rear duplex scales, and a Renner action, among other features. The Magnetic Balanced Action feature (see page 233 of *The Piano Book*) will be available as an option. Also being introduced soon is a new 53" vertical model P135. It will have a Renner action, full sostenuto, a soft-close fallboard, and a newly-designed adjustable music desk, among other features.

PIANODISC

PianoDisc has replaced the PDS 128 Plus system with the 228 CFX. The main difference is that the 228 CFX has both a floppy drive and a CD drive as standard equipment, so it is unnecessary to plug in your own CD player (although you can do so if you have a multi-disc CD changer you want to use). The company says that the control box is the smallest such box with both floppy and CD drives on the market. It can be mounted on the piano or can be located up to 100 feet away and operated with the included infrared wireless remote control.

PianoDisc has introduced an MX Platinum option that utilizes 64 MB of flash memory to store hours of music and play it back without ever having to change a disk. MX Platinum comes with 35 hours of pre-selected music (589 songs), to which one can add music from floppy disks, TFT MIDI Record, and standard MIDI files (but not PianoDisc CDs). PianoDisc's regular MX feature with 32 MB of flash memory still remains available as an option.

PianoDisc has discontinued its GT360 and GT90 QuietTime systems and replaced them with a QuietTime system that includes most of the same components, but without the sound card and control box. The new system, known as GT0 [zero], comes with a power supply, MIDI cable, a MIDI strip for installing under the keys, three pedal switches, a MIDI board with cover, headphones, and a mute rail that, when activated, prevents the hammers from hitting the strings. Customers can buy and use any off-the-shelf sound module with the system.

PianoDisc has introduced a new remote control called the PianoDisc Home Theater Master. It features an LCD touch screen and eliminates the need to have multiple remote controls to operate other various electronic devices. This remote is specially programmed to operate the PianoDisc and can be programmed to control eleven other Audio and Video components including: Stereo, CD, Tape, CATV, Satellite, TV, DVD, VCR and Laser Disc.

PLEYEL

Web site address: www.pleyel.fr

The company says it plans to introduce a 5' 7" grand in early 2002.

PRAMBERGER

See "Young Chang"

RIDGEWOOD

The Ridgewood name is no longer being applied to vertical pianos except, occasionally, on a Dongbei model 112 that normally bears the Sagenhaft name. Ridgewood grands are now being made by Dongbei, and only in 5' and 5' 5" sizes; the 5' 2" and 7' models have been discontinued.

RIEGER-KLOSS

Additional web site address: www.bohemiapiano.com

Rieger-Kloss is gradually shifting all its manufacturing to its Czech facility. For awhile, however, the grands will include a mixture of Young Chang and Czech-made strung backs. New 6' 11" and 8' 11" grands have been introduced, the latter available by special order only. All vertical models smaller than 48" have been discontinued.

SAGENHAFT

The product line has been trimmed down to only the 44½" model 112 vertical.

SAMICK

Samick has purchased the Knabe name and has plans to put the name on a premium-level piano at some point in the future.

SAUTER

Additional web site address: www.sauter-pianos.de

Sauter has introduced a new 44" model 112 with adjustable feet for leveling the piano or for making the piano fit securely on an unlevel floor. There is also a quite beautiful new Peter Maly–designed version of the 48" model with butterfly lids.

SCHIMMEL

New address for U.S. distributor:

Schimmel Piano Corporation
577B Hackman Road
Lititz, Pennsylvania 17543

Schimmel has developed several new upright models based on a more traditional philosphy of construction. These are the F 122 (48"), S 125 (49"), and O 132 (52"). Older models in the same or similar sizes continue to be produced, however. In the older models, the plate is the main structural support and contains a pocket for the pinblock. In the new models, traditional back posts assume a greater role for support, and the pinblock and soundboard are attached to the posts. The company says that the joining of wooden structural and acoustical parts enhances the tone. The new models also incorporate duplex scaling.

Schimmel expects to release a new 5' 7" model 169 grand in the summer of 2001. The company says the piano will have the same treble scale and action as its 7' grand, and almost the same size soundboard as its 6' grand. To obtain the larger soundboard, the case sides are angled slightly.

SCHULZE POLLMANN

Schulze Pollmann has introduced a new 5' 3" model 160 grand. It comes with a Detoa action, but can be ordered with a Renner action at additional cost. The 46" model 117 vertical has a new scale design with agraffes and has been redesignated as model 118. The 50" model 126E has been similarly redesigned and is now called 126P6.

SEILER

The 6' 9" grand model 206 has been redesigned with a duplex scale, longer keys, and a lighter touch, and has been redesignated as model 208. The 8' model 240 has likewise received a duplex scale and lighter touch.

The distributor says that if there is no Seiler dealer in the customer's area, the customer may be able to purchase a Seiler piano directly from the distributor.

SOHMER

The Sohmer name has been purchased from Mason & Hamlin by an unnamed party. However, plans have not yet been made for how the name will be used.

STECK, GEORGE

PianoDisc has discontinued its George Steck line of PianoDisc-equipped, Chinese-made pianos, and has sold the George Steck name to another party. No plans have yet been made for the name's future use.

STEINBERG, WILH.

The name of the manufacturer has changed from Wilhelm Steinberg Pianofortefabrik Gmbh to Thüringer Pianoforte GmbH. The company has also sold its key-making business to Kluge, now part of Steinway.

A new 47" model C2 vertical has a simpler cabinet than the company's IQ models. Steinberg says it will not be making the 49" vertical available with a Fandrich action, as mentioned in *The Piano Book.*

The warranty has been changed to five years, parts and labor.

Correction: *The Piano Book* says that the Wilh. Steinberg grand is identical to the Steingraeber grand. Although the Steinberg grand evolved from the Steingraeber, unlike the Steingraeber, the Steinberg has a duplex scale, as well as a different method of rim construction and a different bridge design.

STEINER, BERNHARD

Web site address: www.bernhardsteiner.com

STEINGRAEBER & SOHNE

Additional web site address: www.steingraeber.de

STORY & CLARK

Web site address: www.storyandclark.com

Story & Clark has made some changes to its grand lineup: 5' and 5' 4" Prelude grands are from the Chinese maker Dongbei; 4' 10", 5' 2", and 5' 6" Cambridge grands are from Beijing; and the 4' 7" and 5' 1" Story & Clark grands made by Samick have been discontinued. Also, a 46" Prelude studio vertical from Dongbei has been added to the line.

STRAUSS

Web site address: www.strausspiano.com

A new 46½" model UP-118 vertical I saw at a trade show sounded, played, and looked much better than previous models I have seen from this company.

WALTER, CHARLES R.

Web site address: walterpiano.com

Walter says he has made some changes to his vertical pianos to better control tuning pin torque (tightness), to reduce the incidence of false beats in the treble, and to smooth out the break between tenor and bass.

WEBER

Weber has introduced a number of "special edition" grand and vertical models. The "WSG" grand models—5' 1", 5' 7", and 6' 1"—have tapered soundboards, "best quality" Young Chang actions, and cosmetic enhancements. The "WSF" and "WSE" 43½" and 48" verticals have cosmetic and action enhancements and the 43½" has a slow-fall fallboard.

Weber has added two more Chinese-made grands to its line, 5' 2" and 5' 9". These are made in Young Chang's Tianjin factory.

WHELPDALE, MAXWELL & CODD

This company has been renamed The British Piano Manufacturing Company Ltd. See under that name for more information.

WOODCHESTER

Additional web site address: www.uk-piano.org/woodchester

Woodchester has been purchased by Whelpdale, Maxwell & Codd, now called The British Piano Manufacturing Company Ltd. See under that name for more information. However, the U.S. contact for Woodchester remains the same as before.

YAMAHA

including Disklavier

Yamaha is now selling a less expensive, Indonesian-made version of its 4' 11" model GA1 grand, in addition to the more expensive model from

Japan. According to Yamaha, the quality of the new model GA1E is at least as good as the Japanese model, and the company encourages buyers to purchase the less expensive one.

Grand model C3 and its Disklavier counterpart DC3A are now available in a "NEO" cabinet style—a modernistic case with an acrylic lid, silver plate, and cherry legs.

The "A" at the end of most Disklavier model designations refers to the new CD (audio) function in these instruments. Disklavier grands are no longer available without the CD function, except for models DGP1 and DGA1, which do not include it. On Disklavier verticals, however, the CD function is not standard, but can be added. DCD1 is an add-on CD drive that can be added to any Disklavier grand or vertical, new or old.

Disklavier Pro models now have all the Mark III Disklavier features (except built-in speakers), including the CD drive, 16 MB of flash memory, and SmartKey and CueTime.

YOUNG CHANG

Young Chang says it has changed the front duplex scale on all its grand models to a new configuration for a cleaner sound.

All Bergmann model numbers now begin with "B," the grands with "BTG." A new 5' 9" model BTG-175 made in China is based on the scale of the Young Chang "Gold" series 5' 9" piano from Korea. A new 43" model BAF-110 is the model BAF-108 with a nicer cabinet.

The Pramberger "Platinum Edition" series now includes a 52" model JP-52 upright.

MODEL and PRICING GUIDE

This guide contains the "list price" for nearly every brand, model, style, and finish of new piano that has regular distribution in the United States and, for the most part, Canada. Some marginal, local, or "stencil" brands are omitted. Except where indicated, prices are in U.S. dollars and the pianos are assumed to be for sale in the U.S. (Canadians will find the information useful after translation into Canadian dollars, but there may be differences in import duties and sales practices that will affect retail prices.) Prices and specifications are, of course, subject to change. Most manufacturers revise their prices at least once a year; two or three times a year is not uncommon when currency exchange rates are unstable. The prices in this edition were compiled in the spring of 2001.

Some terms used in this guide require special explanation and disclaimers:

List Price

The list price is usually a starting point for negotiation, not a final sales price. The term "list price," as used in this *Supplement*, is a "standard" list price computed from the published wholesale price according to a formula commonly used in the industry. Some manufacturers use a different formula, however, for their own suggested retail prices, usually one that raises the prices above "standard" list by ten to fifteen percent so that their dealers can advertise a larger "discount" without losing profit. For this reason, price-shopping by comparing discounts from the manufacturers' own suggested retail prices may result in a faulty price comparison. To provide a level playing field for comparing prices, all prices in this guide are computed according to a uniform "standard" formula, *even though it may differ from the manufacturers' own suggested retail prices.* Where my list prices and those of a manufacturer differ, then, no dishonesty should be inferred; we simply employ different formulas. For most brands, but not all, the price includes a bench and the standard manufacturer's warranty for that brand (see *The Piano Book* for details). Prices for some European brands do not include a bench. Most dealers will also include moving and one or two tunings in the home, but these are optional and a matter of agreement between you and the dealer.

Style and Finish

Unless otherwise indicated, the cabinet style is assumed to be "traditional" and is not stated. Exactly what "traditional" means varies from brand to brand. In general, it is a "classic" styling with minimal embellishment and straight legs. The vertical pianos have front legs, which are free-standing on smaller verticals and attached to the cabinet with toe blocks on larger verticals. "Continental" or European styling refers to vertical pianos without decorative trim and usually without front legs. Other furniture styles (Chippendale, French Provincial, Queen Anne, etc.) are as noted. The manufacturer's own trademarked style name is used when an appropriate generic name could not be determined.

Unless otherwise stated, all finishes are assumed to be "satin," which reflects light but not images. "Polished" finishes, also known as "high-gloss" or "high-polish," are mirror-like. "Oiled" finishes are usually matte (not shiny). "Open-pore" finishes, common on some European pianos, are slightly "grainier" satin finishes due to the wood pores not being filled in prior to finishing. In fact, many finishes labeled "satin" on European pianos are actually open-pore. "Ebony" is a black finish.

Special-order–only styles and finishes are in italics.

Some descriptions of style and finish may be slightly different from the manufacturer's own for the purpose of clarity, consistency, saving space, or other reason.

Size

The height of a vertical piano is measured from the floor to the top of the piano. The length of a grand piano is measured from the very front (keyboard end) to the very back (tail end).

About Actual Selling or "Street" Prices

Buying a piano is something like buying a car—the list price is deliberately set high in anticipation of negotiating.* But sometimes this is carried to extremes, as when the salesperson reduces the price three times in the first fifteen minutes to barely half the sticker price. In situations like this, the customer, understandably confused, is bound to ask in exasperation, "What is the *real* price of this piano?"

---

* A relatively small number of dealers have non-negotiable prices.

Unfortunately, there *is* no "real" price. In theory, the dealer pays a wholesale price and then marks it up by an amount sufficient to cover the overhead and produce a profit. In practice, however, the markup can vary considerably from sale to sale depending on such factors as:

- how long the inventory has been sitting around, racking up finance charges for the dealer
- how much of a discount the dealer received at the wholesale level for buying in quantity or for paying cash
- the dealer's cash flow situation
- the competition in that particular geographic area for a particular brand or type of piano
- special piano sales events taking place in the area
- how the salesperson sizes up your situation and your willingness to pay
- the level of pre- and post-sale service the dealer seeks to provide
- the dealer's other overhead expenses

It's not unusual for one person to pay fifty percent more than another for the same brand and model of piano—sometimes even from the same dealer on the same day! It may seem as if pricing is so chaotic that no advice can be given, but in truth, enough piano sales do fall within a certain range of typical profit margins that some guidance is possible as long as the reader understands the limitations inherent in this kind of advice.

Historically, discounts from "standard" list price have averaged ten or fifteen percent in the piano business. In recent years, however, conditions have changed such that, according to some industry sources, the average discount from list has increased to twenty or twenty-five percent. Essentially, due to growing competition from used pianos and digital pianos, and a decrease in the cultural importance attached to having a piano in the home, there are too many dealers of new pianos chasing after too few consumer dollars. In addition, higher labor costs worldwide and unfavorable international currency values make some brands so expensive in the U.S. that they can only be sold at very large discounts. I think, too, that consumers are becoming more savvy and are shopping around. Unfortunately, the overhead costs of running a traditional piano store are so high that most dealers cannot stay in business if they sell at an average discount from "standard" list price of more than about twenty percent. To survive, dealers are evolving multiple new approaches: becoming more efficient, instituting low-price/high volume strategies, cutting their overhead—sometimes including service—or subsidizing their meager sales of new pianos with used pianos (which command higher profit margins), rentals, rebuilding, and other products and services.

Although the average discount has increased, it is by no means uniform. Some brands dependably bring top dollar; others languish or the price is highly situational. I did consider giving a typical range of "street" prices for each brand and model listed in this volume, but concluded that the task would be too daunting due to the extreme variation that can exist from one situation to another, and because of the political fallout that would likely result from dealers and manufacturers who fear the loss of what little power they still have over aggressive, price-shopping customers. So, for now, I've decided just to give general advice in print. (For those who desire more specific information on "street" prices, I offer additional services, such as private telephone consultations and a Pricing Guide Service on the internet. See my web site, **www.pianobook.com**, for more information.)

It should be clearly understood that the advice given here is based on my own observations, subjective judgment, and general understanding of the piano market, *not* on statistical sales data or scientific analysis. (Brand-by-brand statistical sales data are virtually nonexistent.) This knowledge is the product of discussions with hundreds of customers, dealers, technicians, and industry executives over the years. Other industry observers may come to different conclusions. This rundown of "street" prices won't cover every brand, but should give a rough idea of what to expect and the ability to predict prices for some of the brands not specifically covered. I can't emphasize enough, however, that pricing can be highly situational, dependent on the mix of available products and the ease of comparison shopping in any particular geographic area, as well as on the financial situation of dealer and customer. The following generalizations should prove useful to you, but expect almost anything.

As a general rule of thumb:

- the more expensive the piano, the higher the possible discount
- the more "exclusive" a brand is perceived to be, the less likely head-to-head competition, and therefore the lower the possible discount

- the longer a piano remains unsold, the higher the possible discount
- the more service-intensive the piano, the lower the possible discount

Although discounts from "standard" list price for Japanese and Korean pianos typically start at perhaps fifteen percent, twenty or even thirty percent discounts are not uncommon in a moderately competitive environment, especially if the dealer knows the customer is shopping around. Korean pianos are disadvantaged by the presence in the market of too many different brand names made by the same two companies, driving prices down. Some Korean pianos—particularly Young Chang products—are sold at large discounts (ten percent or more) from the published *wholesale* price to dealers who buy in sufficient quantity or for certain models, a savings the dealers can pass on to the retail customers if they choose to do so or if they must do so to compete. (Many manufacturers do this to some extent or from time to time, but Young Chang seems to have a more consistent policy about it.) The problem for the consumer is that these wholesale discounts are not given out uniformly among dealers, so figuring out an appropriate "street" price for a particular dealer, model, and situation from the price information presented in this *Supplement* could be difficult.

The Boston piano, although manufactured in Japan, is generally viewed as being a little more "exclusive" due to its association with Steinway, so deep discounting is much less likely. Discounts in the range of ten percent or so are common. Baldwin, whose pianos are usually seen as being distinctly different from the Asian products even though they often share common price ranges, also benefits from exceptional name recognition and its historical "made in USA" connection. Discounting is likely to be moderate, in my experience—perhaps fifteen to twenty-five percent.

Western European instruments tend to be extremely expensive here due to their high quality, the high European cost of doing business, additional middlemen/importers and, sometimes, unfavorable exchange rates. There appear to be two types of dealers of these pianos. One type, specializing in selling higher-quality instruments to a demanding clientele, manages to get top dollar for them despite their high price, with discounts averaging only twenty percent or so. They are not particularly into negotiating. The other type of dealer, probably more numerous, depends for his or her "bread and butter" on consumer-grade pianos and is pleased to make a relatively small profit on the occasional sale of a luxury instrument. Discounts here may well approach thirty to forty percent at times, especially if the piano has gone unsold for an extended period of time. Eastern European brands like Petrof and Estonia are already seen as being a good deal for the money and are more service-intensive for the dealer than those from Western Europe, so expect moderate discounts—perhaps fifteen to twenty-five percent.

At the other end of the price spectrum, most Russian and Chinese pianos are so cheap, and require so much servicing by the dealer, that it's simply not cost-effective to sell them for much less than full list price. However, some dealers do use them as "loss leaders," that is, just to get people into the store, whereupon the customer is sold on a more expensive piano. In that situation, the occasional customer who actually chooses to buy the "leader" may do so at a large discount.

Steinway pianos have always been in a class by themselves, historically the only expensive piano to continually command high profit margins. Except for older Steinways and the occasional Mason & Hamlin, Steinway has little competition and fewer than one hundred dealers in the United States. Service requirements can be quite high, at least in part because of the higher standards often required to satisfy a fussier clientele. Historically, Steinway pianos have sold at or near full list price. (Some dealers even sell *above* list!) This is still true in many places, but in recent years I have seen a little more discounting than in the past. Ten to fifteen percent is not unusual in some areas; as much as twenty percent would be rare.

For brands not mentioned or implied in the above discussion, it's usually a safe bet to figure a discount of fifteen to twenty-five percent from the prices in this *Supplement*, with greater discounts possible in selected situations.

There is no "fair" price for a piano except the one the buyer and seller agree on. The dealer is no more obligated to sell you a piano at a deep discount than you are obligated to pay the list price. Many dealers are simply not able to sell at the low end of the range consistently and still stay in business. It's understandable that you would like to pay the lowest price possible, and there's no harm in asking, but remember that piano shopping is not just about chasing the lowest price. Be sure you are getting the instrument that best suits your needs and preferences and that the dealer is committed to providing the proper pre- and post-sale service.

(Note: Remember that the "street" price discounts suggested above should be subtracted from the "standard" list prices in this *Supplement*, not from the manufacturer's suggested retail price.)

For more information on shopping for a new piano and on how to save money, please see pages 60–75 in *The Piano Book* (fourth edition).

Model	Size	Style and Finish	Price*

Albrecht, Charles

Verticals

4300	43"	Contemporary Polished Ebony	3,860.
4300	43"	Contemporary Polished Mahogany	3,960.
4300	43"	Contemporary Walnut	3,660.
4300	43"	Contemporary Polished Walnut	3,960.
4300	43"	Contemporary Cherry	3,660.
4300	43"	Contemporary Polished Ivory	3,960.
4300	43"	Contemporary Polished White	3,960.
4401	44"	Designer Cherry	4,260.
4401	44"	Designer Mahogany	4,260.
4403	44"	Designer Cherry	4,260.
4403	44"	Designer Brown Oak	4,260.
4406	44"	Designer Brown Oak	4,160.
4507	45"	Institutional Polished Ebony	4,060.
4507	45"	Institutional Polished Mahogany	4,160.
4507	45"	Institutional Polished Walnut	4,160.
4507	45"	Institutional Cherry	3,860.
4507	45"	Institutional Walnut	3,860.
4507	45"	Institutional Polished Ivory	4,160.
4507	45"	Institutional Polished White	4,160.
4701	47"	Designer Cherry	4,860.
4701	47"	Designer Mahogany	4,860.
4703	47"	Designer Cherry	4,860.
4703	47"	Designer Mahogany	4,860.
4706	47"	Designer Brown Oak	4,660.
4803	48"	Institutional Polished Ebony	4,860.
4803	48"	Institutional Polished Mahogany	5,260.
4907	49"	Institutional Polished Ebony	5,220.
4907	49"	Institutional Polished Mahogany	5,220.
4907	49"	Institutional Polished Walnut	5,220.
5207	52"	Institutional Ebony or Polished Ebony	6,260.
5207	52"	Institutional Polished Mahogany	6,460.
5207	52"	Institutional Polished Walnut	6,460.
5207	52"	Institutional Polished Ivory	6,260.

Model	Size	Style and Finish	Price*
Grands			
G4701	4' 7"	"Petite" Polished Ebony	8,360.
G4701	4' 7"	"Petite" Polished White	8,760.
G5001	5'	Polished Ebony	8,470.
G5101	5'1"	Polished Ebony	11,260.
G5101	5'1"	Walnut or Polished Walnut	11,760.
G5101	5'1"	Polished Mahogany	11,760.
G5101	5'1"	Polished Ivory	11,260.
G5101	5'1"	Polished White	11,260.
G5209	5' 2-1/2"	Victorian Polished Ebony	10,460.
G5209	5' 2-1/2"	Victorian Polished Mahogany	10,660.
G5209	5' 2-1/2"	Victorian Polished Walnut	10,660.

Astin-Weight

Verticals			
375	41"	Santa Fe Oiled Oak	8,740.
375	41"	Spanish Oiled Oak	7,980.
375	41"	Spanish Lacquer Oak	8,180.
375	41"	Italian Oiled Walnut	8,380.
375	41"	Italian Lacquer Walnut	8,580.
375	41"	Regency Oiled Oak	8,380.
375	41"	Regency Lacquer Oak	8,500.
375	41"	Regency Oiled Walnut	8,500.
375	41"	Regency Lacquer Walnut	8,520.
U-500	50"	Oiled Oak	13,380.
U-500	50"	Santa Fe Oiled Oak	14,780.
U-500	50"	Lacquer Oak	13,780.
U-500	50"	Oiled Walnut	13,980.
U-500	50"	Lacquer Walnut	14,380.
Grands			
———	5' 9"	Ebony	35,700.

August Förster — see "Förster, August"

***For explanation of terms and prices, please see pages 20–25.**

Model	Size	Style and Finish	Price*

Bachendorff

Verticals

RC-115S	44"	Ebony and Polished Ebony	8,760.
RC-115S	44"	Walnut and Polished Walnut	9,160.
RC-115S	44"	Mahogany and Polished Mahogany	9,160.
RC-115S	44"	Cherry and Polished Cherry	9,260.
RC-115S	44"	*Polished Oak*	9,260.
RC-115S	44"	*Polished White*	9,260.
RC-115A	44"	Ebony and Polished Ebony	9,540.
RC-115A	44"	Walnut and Polished Walnut	9,940.
RC-115A	44"	Mahogany and Polished Mahogany	9,940.
RC-115A	44"	Cherry and Polished Cherry	10,040.
RC-115A	44"	*Polished Oak*	10,040.
RC-115A	44"	*Polished White*	10,040.
CF-115	44"	Mediterranean Ebony and Pol. Ebony	7,500.
CF-115	44"	Mediterranean Walnut and Pol. Walnut	7,900.
CF-115	44"	Mediterranean Mahog. and Pol. Mahog.	7,900.
CF-115	44"	Mediterranean Cherry and Pol. Cherry	8,000.
CS-115	44"	Italian Provincial Ebony and Pol. Ebony	7,500.
CS-115	44"	Italian Provin. Walnut and Pol. Walnut	7,900.
CS-115	44"	Italian Provin. Mahog. and Pol. Mahog.	7,900.
CS-115	44"	Italian Provin. Cherry and Pol. Cherry	8,000.
CR-115	44"	Queen Anne Ebony and Polished Ebony	7,500.
CR-115	44"	Queen Anne Walnut and Pol. Walnut	7,900.
CR-115	44"	Queen Anne Mahog. and Pol. Mahog.	7,900.
CR-115	44"	Queen Anne Cherry and Pol. Cherry	8,000.
115SE	44"	Ebony and Polished Ebony	6,480.
115SE	44"	Walnut and Polished Walnut	6,880.
115SE	44"	Mahogany and Polished Mahogany	6,880.
115SE	44"	Cherry and Polished Cherry	6,980.
115AE	44"	Ebony and Polished Ebony	7,140.
115AE	44"	Walnut and Polished Walnut	7,500.
115AE	44"	Mahogany and Polished Mahogany	7,500.
115AE	44"	Cherry and Polished Cherry	7,600.
RC-122S	48"	Ebony and Polished Ebony	9,920.
RC-122S	48"	Walnut and Polished Walnut	10,320.

Model	Size	Style and Finish	Price*
RC-122S	48"	Mahogany and Polished Mahogany	10,320.
RC-122S	48"	Cherry and Polished Cherry	10,420.
RC-122S	48"	*Polished Oak*	10,420.
RC-122S	48"	*Polished White*	10,420.
RC-122A	48"	Ebony and Polished Ebony	10,320.
RC-122A	48"	Walnut and Polished Walnut	10,720.
RC-122A	48"	Mahogany and Polished Mahogany	10,720.
RC-122A	48"	Cherry and Polished Cherry	10,820.
RC-122A	48"	*Polished Oak*	10,820.
RC-122A	48"	*Polished White*	10,820.
RC-128S	50"	Ebony and Polished Ebony	10,700.
RC-128S	50"	Walnut and Polished Walnut	11,100.
RC-128S	50"	Mahogany and Polished Mahogany	11,100.
RC-128S	50"	Cherry and Polished Cherry	11,200.
RC-128S	50"	*Polished Oak*	11,200.
RC-128S	50"	*Polished White*	11,200.
Grands			
RC-160	5' 4"	Ebony and Polished Ebony	25,940.
RC-160	5' 4"	Walnut and Polished Walnut	27,140.
RC-160	5' 4"	Mahogany and Polished Mahogany	27,140.
RC-160	5' 4"	Cherry and Polished Cherry	27,340.
RC-180	6'	Ebony and Polished Ebony	29,940.
RC-180	6'	Walnut and Polished Walnut	31,540.
RC-180	6'	Mahogany and Polished Mahogany	31,540.
RC-180	6'	Cherry and Polished Cherry	31,740.
RC-215	7'	Ebony and Polished Ebony	34,400.
RC-215	7'	Walnut and Polished Walnut	36,200.
RC-215	7'	Mahogany and Polished Mahogany	36,200.
RC-215	7'	Cherry and Polished Cherry	36,400.

Baldwin

Verticals			
660	43-1/2"	Georgian Mahogany	4,510.
662	43-1/2"	Queen Anne Regency Cherry	4,510.
665	43-1/2"	Transitional Country Oak	4,510.
667	43-1/2"	Country French Oak	4,510.

***For explanation of terms and prices, please see pages 20–25.**

Model	Size	Style and Finish	Price*
Baldwin (continued)			
2090	43-1/2"	Hepplewhite Vintage Mahogany	5,270.
2095	43-1/2"	Regal Oak	5,270.
2096	43-1/2"	Queen Anne Royal Cherry	5,270.
E101	44"	Continental Polished Ebony	5,500.
E101	44"	Continental Polished White	5,900.
E102	45"	Polished Ebony	5,790.
E102	45"	Polished Mahogany	6,190.
243HPA	45"	Ebony	5,550.
243HPA	45"	Golden Oak	5,340.
243HPA	45"	American Walnut	5,540.
5050A	45"	Limited Edition Mahogany	7,310.
5052A	45"	Limited Edition Queen Anne Cherry	7,310.
5057B	45"	Limited Edition Georgian Oak	7,310.
E260	45"	Contemporary Polished Ebony	6,500.
E260	45"	Contemporary Polished Mahogany	6,900.
248A	48"	Polished Ebony	7,970.
248A	48"	American Walnut	7,970.
6000	52"	Ebony	10,310.
6000	52"	Mahogany	10,540.
Grands			
M1	5' 2"	Ebony	25,100.
M1	5' 2"	Polished Ebony	26,100.
M1	5' 2"	Mahogany	26,000.
M1	5' 2"	Polished Mahogany	27,950.
M1	5' 2"	Walnut	26,700.
M1	5' 2"	Polished Cherry	27,640.
225E	5' 2"	French Provincial Cherry	31,560.
R1	5' 8"	Ebony	28,240.
R1	5' 8"	Polished Ebony	29,400.
R1	5' 8"	Mahogany	29,460.
R1	5' 8"	Polished Mahogany	31,410.
R1	5' 8"	Walnut	30,260.
R1	5' 8"	Polished Cherry	31,320.
226E	5' 8"	French Provincial Royal Cherry	34,800.
226E	5' 8"	French Provincial Polished Cherry	36,000.

Model	Size	Style and Finish	Price*
227E	5' 8"	Louis XVI Mahogany	34,800.
L1	6' 3"	Ebony	31,880.
L1	6' 3"	Polished Ebony	33,080.
L1	6' 3"	Mahogany	33,200.
L1	6' 3"	Polished Mahogany	35,200.
L1	6' 3"	Walnut	34,200.
L1	6' 3"	Polished Cherry	35,320.
SF10E	7'	Ebony	44,840.
SF10E	7'	Polished Ebony	46,300.
SD10	9'	Ebony	71,700.
SD10	9'	Polished Ebony	76,720.
ConcertMaster (approximate, including installation by factory or dealer)			
Verticals		Playback only / with Perf. Option	8,520./9,730.
Grands		Playback only / with Perf. Option	9,200./10,500.
		With stop rail, add $400	

Note: Discounts may apply, especially as an incentive to purchase the piano.

Bechstein, C.

Verticals

Balance 116	45-1/2"	Ebony	18,920.
Balance 116	45-1/2"	Polished Ebony	19,340.
Advance 118	46-1/2"	Ebony	21,840.
Advance 118	46-1/2"	Polished Ebony	22,440.
Classic 118	47"	Ebony	17,980.
Classic 118	47"	Polished Ebony	18,960.
Classic 118	47"	Walnut	18,440.
Classic 118	47"	Mahogany	18,440.
Classic 118	47"	Cherry	18,960.
Classic 118	47"	Oak	18,440.
Classic 118	47"	Beech	17,980.
Classic 118	47"	Polished Woods (above)	20,000.
Classic 118	47"	Polished White	20,000.
Contour 118	47"	Polished Ebony	19,840.
Contour 118	47"	Walnut	19,440.
Contour 118	47"	Mahogany	19,440.
Contour 118	47"	Cherry	19,840.

***For explanation of terms and prices, please see pages 20–25.**

Model	Size	Style and Finish	Price*

Bechstein, C. (continued)

Model	Size	Style and Finish	Price*
Contour 118	47"	Oak	19,440.
Contour 118	47"	Alder	18,660.
Contour 118	47"	Polished Woods (above)	20,880.
Contour 118	47"	Polished White	20,880.
Classic 124	49"	Polished Ebony	24,000.
Classic 124	49"	Walnut	23,600.
Classic 124	49"	Mahogany	23,600.
Classic 124	49"	Cherry	24,000.
Classic 124	49"	Oak	23,600.
Classic 124	49"	Polished Woods (above)	24,860.
Classic 124	49"	Polished White	24,860.
Elegance 124	49"	Polished Ebony	25,060.
Elegance 124	49"	Walnut	25,060.
Elegance 124	49"	Mahogany	25,060.
Elegance 124	49"	Cherry	25,060.
Elegance 124	49"	Oak	25,060.
Elegance 124	49"	Polished Woods (above)	26,120.
Elegance 124	49"	Polished White	26,120.
Ars Nova 124	49"	Ebony	26,320.
Ars Nova 124	49"	Polished Ebony	26,940.
Concert 11	50"	Polished Ebony	31,660.
Concert 11	50"	Walnut	30,920.
Concert 11	50"	Mahogany	30,920.
Concert 11	50"	Cherry	30,920.
Concert 11	50"	Polished Woods (above)	32,300.
Concert 11	50"	Polished White	32,300.
Concert 8	52"	Polished Ebony	34,880.
Concert 8	52"	Walnut	34,040.
Concert 8	52"	Mahogany	34,040.
Concert 8	52"	Cherry	34,040.
Concert 8	52"	Polished Woods (above)	35,640.
Concert 8	52"	Polished White	35,640.
Concert 8	52"	*Add for sostenuto*	2,960.

Model	Size	Style and Finish	Price*
Grands			
K-158	5' 2"	Polished Ebony	58,480.
K-158	5' 2"	Mahogany	56,400.
K-158	5' 2"	Oak	56,400.
K-158	5' 2"	Walnut	58,480.
K-158	5' 2"	Cherry	58,480.
K-158	5' 2"	Polished Woods (above)	59,740.
K-158	5' 2"	Polished White	59,740.
K-158	5' 2"	Yew	59,740.
K-158	5' 2"	Classic Polished Ebony	66,840.
K-158	5' 2"	Classic Mahogany	64,760.
K-158	5' 2"	Classic Oak	64,760.
K-158	5' 2"	Classic Walnut	66,840.
K-158	5' 2"	Classic Cherry	66,840.
K-158	5' 2"	Classic Polished Woods (above)	68,100.
K-158	5' 2"	Classic Polished White	68,100.
K-158	5' 2"	Classic Yew	68,100.
M-180	5' 11"	Polished Ebony	63,920.
M-180	5' 11"	Mahogany	61,820.
M-180	5' 11"	Oak	61,820.
M-180	5' 11"	Walnut	63,920.
M-180	5' 11"	Cherry	63,920.
M-180	5' 11"	Polished Woods (above)	66,000.
M-180	5' 11"	Polished White	66,000.
M-180	5' 11"	Yew	66,000.
M-180	5' 11"	Polished Pyramid Mahogany	73,740.
M-180	5' 11"	Polished Mahogany with Inlays	76,860.
M-180	5' 11"	Classic Polished Ebony	72,250.
M-180	5' 11"	Classic Mahogany	70,080.
M-180	5' 11"	Classic Oak	70,080.
M-180	5' 11"	Classic Walnut	72,250.
M-180	5' 11"	Classic Cherry	72,250.
M-180	5' 11"	Classic Polished Woods (above)	74,340.
M-180	5' 11"	Classic Polished White	74,340.
M-180	5' 11"	Classic Yew	74,340.
M-180	5' 11"	Classic Polished Burled Walnut	82,180.
M-180	5' 11"	Classic Polished Varvona	82,180.

***For explanation of terms and prices, please see pages 20–25.**

Model	Size	Style and Finish	Price*

Bechstein, C. (continued)

Model	Size	Style and Finish	Price*
A-189	6' 2"	"Academy" Ebony	48,780.
A-189	6' 2"	Polished Ebony	57,440.
A-189	6' 2"	Oak	54,300.
A-189	6' 2"	Walnut	54,300.
A-189	6' 2"	Polished Walnut	58,280.
A-189	6' 2"	Cherry	54,300.
A-189	6' 2"	Polished Mahogany	58,280.
A-189	6' 2"	Polished White	58,280.
A-189	6' 2"	Polished Pyramid Mahogany	68,300.
A-189	6' 2"	Polished Mahogany with Inlays	69,560.
A-189	6' 2"	Classic Polished Ebony	66,000.
A-189	6' 2"	Classic Oak	62,660.
A-189	6' 2"	Classic Walnut	62,660.
A-189	6' 2"	Classic Polished Walnut	67,040.
A-189	6' 2"	Classic Cherry	62,660.
A-189	6' 2"	Classic Polished Mahogany	67,040.
A-189	6' 2"	Classic Polished White	67,040.
A-189	6' 2"	Classic Polished Burled Walnut	76,240.
A-189	6' 2"	Classic Polished Varvona	76,240.
B-208	6' 10"	"Academy" Ebony	70,680.
B-208	6' 10"	Polished Ebony	80,100.
B-208	6' 10"	Mahogany	80,100.
B-208	6' 10"	Oak	80,100.
B-208	6' 10"	Walnut	80,100.
B-208	6' 10"	Cherry	80,100.
B-208	6' 10"	Polished Woods (above)	83,220.
B-208	6' 10"	Classic Polished Ebony	89,600.
B-208	6' 10"	Classic Mahogany	89,600.
B-208	6' 10"	Classic Oak	89,600.
B-208	6' 10"	Classic Walnut	89,600.
B-208	6' 10"	Classic Cherry	89,600.
B-208	6' 10"	Classic Polished Woods (above)	91,700.
C-232	7' 6"	Polished Ebony	94,620.
C-232	7' 6"	Classic Polished Ebony	103,940.
D-280	9' 2"	Polished Ebony	128,160.

Model	Size	Style and Finish	Price*

Becker, J.

Verticals

B-120	46"	Continental Polished Ebony	2,070.
B-120	46"	Continental Polished Mahogany	2,070.
B-120	46"	Continental Polished Oak	2,070.
A-121	47"	"Aurora" Polshed Ebony	2,890.
A-121	47"	"Aurora" Polished Mahogany	2,890.
A-121	47"	"Aurora" Polished Oak	2,890.
A-122	47"	"Aurora" Chippendale Polished Ebony	2,990.
A-122	47"	"Aurora" Chippendale Pol. Mahagony	2,990.
A-122	47"	"Aurora" Chippendale Polished Oak	2,990.
A-122	47"	"Aurora" Chippendale Polished Walnut	2,990.
A-122	47"	"Aurora" Chippendale Polished White	3,100.
A-123 CZ	47"	"Avante" Classic Polished Ebony	3,290.
A-123 CZ	47"	"Avante" Classic Polished Mahogany	3,290.
A-123 CZ	47"	"Avante" Classic Polished Oak	3,290.
A-124 CZ	47"	"Avante" Classic Chippendale Pol. Eby.	3,390.
A-124 CZ	47"	"Avante" Classic Chippendale Pol.Mah.	3,390.
A-124 CZ	47"	"Avante" Classic Chippendale Pol. Oak	3,390.
A-124 CZ	47"	"Avante" Classic Chippendale Pol. Wal.	3,390.
A-124 CZ	47"	"Avante" Classic Chippendale Pol. Wht.	3,500.

Grands

GP-155M	5' 2"	"Mignon" Polished Ebony	7,380.
GP-155M	5' 2"	"Mignon" Polished White	7,580.
GP-155 CZ	5' 2"	"Avante" Polished Ebony	8,780.
GP-155 CZ	5' 2"	"Avante" Polished Mahogany	9,180.
GP-155 CZ	5' 2"	"Avante" Polished White	8,980.

Bentley

Prices are FOB England and do not include duty, freight, and other costs of importing. Oak, ash, and cherry are available at the same price as mahogany. Polished white is available at the same price as polished ebony.

Verticals

Concord	43"	Polished Ebony	7,455.
Concord	43"	Mahogany	6,165.

***For explanation of terms and prices, please see pages 20–25.**

Model	Size	Style and Finish	Price*

Bentley (continued)

Model	Size	Style and Finish	Price*
Concord	43"	Polished Mahogany	7,455.
Concord	43"	Walnut	6,165.
Concord	43"	Polished Walnut	7,455.
Concord	43"	Teak	6,165.
Concord	43"	Chippendale Mahogany	6,525.
Concord	43"	Chippendale Polished Mahogany	8,025.
Concord	43"	Chippendale Walnut	6,525.
Concord	43"	Chippendale Polished Walnut	8,025.
Heritage	43"	Mahogany	6,750.
Heritage	43"	Polished Mahogany	7,860.
Wessex	46"	Polished Ebony	7,950.
Wessex	46"	Mahogany	6,750.
Wessex	46"	Polished Mahogany	7,950.
Wessex	46"	Walnut	6,750.
Wessex	46"	Polished Walnut	7,950.
Berkeley	46"	Mahogany	7,485.
Berkeley	46"	Polished Mahogany	8,730.
Exeter	47"	Polished Ebony	8,760.
Exeter	47"	Mahogany	7,590.
Exeter	47"	Polished Mahogany	8,760.
Exeter	47"	Walnut	7,590.
Exeter	47"	Polished Walnut	8,760.
Berlin	47"	Polished Ebony	8,925.
Berlin	47"	Mahogany	7,935.
Berlin	47"	Polished Mahogany	8,925.
Berlin	47"	Walnut	7,935.
Berlin	47"	Polished Walnut	8,925.
London	47"	Mahogany	8,355.
London	47"	Polished Mahogany	9,405.
Belgrave	47"	Mahogany	8,355.
Belgrave	47"	Polished Mahogany	9,405.
Chelsea	47"	Mahogany	8,355.
Chelsea	47"	Polished Mahogany	9,405.
Salisbury	47"	Mahogany	8,400.
Salisbury	47"	Polished Mahogany	9,450.

Model	Size	Style and Finish	Price*
Salisbury	47"	Walnut	8,400.
Salisbury	47"	Polished Walnut	9,450.
Esher	47"	Mahogany	8,700.
Esher	47"	Polished Mahogany	9,825.
Esher	47"	Walnut	8,700.
Esher	47"	Polished Walnut	9,825.

Bergmann

Verticals			
BE-109	43"	Continental Polished Ebony	2,700.
BE-109	43"	Continental Polished Red Mahogany	2,790.
BE-109	43"	Continental Polished Ivory	2,700.
BAF-108	43"	Mahogany	3,190.
BAF-108	43"	Queen Anne Oak	3,190.
BAF-108	43"	Mediterranean Oak	3,190.
BAF-108	43"	Queen Anne Cherry	3,190.
BAF-108	43"	French Provincial Cherry	3,190.
BAF-110	43-1/2"	Mahogany	3,590.
BAF-110	43-1/2"	Queen Anne Oak	3,590.
BAF-110	43-1/2"	French Provincial Cherry	3,590.
BE-118	47"	Polished Ebony	3,190.
BE-118	47"	Polished Red Mahogany	3,300.
BE-121	48"	Polished Ebony	3,390.
BE-121	48"	Polished Red Mahogany	3,500.
BE-131	52"	Polished Ebony	3,590.
Grands			
BTG-150	4' 11"	Polished Ebony	8,390.
BTG-150	4' 11"	Polished Red Mahogany	8,390.
BTG-150	4' 11"	Polished Ivory	8,390.
BTG-157	5' 2"	Polished Ebony	9,390.
BTG-157	5' 2"	Polished Red Mahogany	9,390.
BTG-157	5' 2"	Polished Ivory	9,390.
BTG-175	5' 9"	Polished Ebony	10,590.

***For explanation of terms and prices, please see pages 20–25.**

Model	Size	Style and Finish	Price*

Blondel, G.

Verticals

Bolero	43"	Ebony	6,680.
Bolero	43"	Polished Ebony	6,780.
Bolero	43"	Mahogany	6,680.
Bolero	43"	Polished Mahogany	6,780.
Bolero	43"	Walnut	6,680.
Bolero	43"	Polished Walnut	6,780.
Bolero	43"	Oak	6,680.
Bolero	43"	Polished Oak	6,780.
Sarabande	47"	Ebony	7,680.
Sarabande	47"	Polished Ebony	7,780.
Sarabande	47"	Mahogany	7,680.
Sarabande	47"	Polished Mahogany	7,780.
Sarabande	47"	Walnut	7,680.
Sarabande	47"	Polished Walnut	7,780.
Sarabande	47"	Oak	7,680.
Sarabande	47"	Polished Oak	7,780.

Grands

Tocata	6' 1"	Ebony	23,680.
Tocata	6' 1"	Polished Ebony	23,780.
Tocata	6' 1"	Mahogany	23,680.
Tocata	6' 1"	Polished Mahogany	23,780.
Tocata	6' 1"	Walnut	23,680.
Tocata	6' 1"	Polished Walnut	23,780.
Tocata	6' 1"	Oak	23,680.
Tocata	6' 1"	Polished Oak	23,780.

Blüthner

Prices do not include bench.

Verticals

I	45"	Ebony or Polished Ebony	17,546.
I	45"	Walnut or Polished Walnut	18,472.
I	45"	Mahogany or Polished Mahogany	18,374.
I	45"	Cherry or Polished Cherry	18,374.

Model	Size	Style and Finish	Price*
I	45"	White or Polished White	18,334.
C	46"	Ebony or Polished Ebony	17,664.
C	46"	Walnut or Polished Walnut	18,688.
C	46"	Mahogany or Polished Mahogany	18,508.
C	46"	Cherry or Polished Cherry	18,598.
C	46"	White or Polished White	18,550.
C	46"	Polished Bubinga, Yew, Macassar Eby.	19,578.
C	46"	Saxony Polished Pyramid Mahogany	23,136.
C	46"	Saxony Polished Burl Walnut Inlay	23,358.
A	49"	Ebony or Polished Ebony	22,500.
A	49"	Walnut or Polished Walnut	23,802.
A	49"	Mahogany or Polished Mahogany	23,574.
A	49"	Cherry or Polished Cherry	23,688.
A	49"	White or Polished White	23,624.
A	49"	Polished Bubinga, Yew, Macassar Eby.	24,934.
A	49"	Saxony Polished Pyramid Mahogany	29,468.
A	49"	Saxony Polished Burl Walnut Inlay	29,752.
B	52"	Ebony or Polished Ebony	25,688.
B	52"	Walnut or Polished Walnut	27,176.
B	52"	Mahogany or Polished Mahogany	26,916.
B	52"	Cherry or Polished Cherry	27,044.
B	52"	White or Polished White	26,974.
B	52"	Polished Bubinga, Yew, Macassar Eby.	28,470.
B	52"	Saxony Polished Pyramid Mahogany	33,644.
B	52"	Saxony Polished Burl Walnut Inlay	33,968.
Grands			
11	5' 1"	Ebony or Polished Ebony	45,554.
11	5' 1"	Walnut or Polished Walnut	48,192.
11	5' 1"	Mahogany or Polished Mahogany	47,678.
11	5' 1"	Cherry or Polished Cherry	47,964.
11	5' 1"	White or Polished White	47,832.
11	5' 1"	Polished Bubinga, Yew, Macassar Eby.	50,486.
11	5' 1"	Saxony Polished Pyramid Mahogany	59,666.
11	5' 1"	Saxony Polished Burl Walnut Inlay	60,240.
11	5' 1"	"President" Polished Ebony	52,368.
11	5' 1"	"President" Polished Mahogany	54,460.
11	5' 1"	"President" Polished Walnut	54,986.

***For explanation of terms and prices, please see pages 20–25.**

Model	Size	Style and Finish	Price*

Blüthner (continued)

11	5' 1"	"President" Polished Bubinga	57,604.
11	5' 1"	Louis XV Ebony or Polished Ebony	54,748.
11	5' 1"	Louis XV Mahogany or Pol. Mahogany	53,502.
11	5' 1"	Louis XV Walnut or Polished Walnut	57,484.
11	5' 1"	"Kaiser Wilhelm II" Polished Ebony	55,224.
11	5' 1"	"Kaiser Wilhelm II" Pol. Mahogany	57,432.
11	5' 1"	"Kaiser Wilhelm II" Polished Walnut	57,986.
11	5' 1"	"Kaiser Wilhelm II" Polished Cherry	57,710.
11	5' 1"	"Ambassador" East Indian Rosewood	64,268.
11	5' 1"	"Ambassador" Walnut	59,508.
11	5' 1"	"Nicolas II" Walnut with Burl Inlay	64,268.
11	5' 1"	Louis XVI Rococo White with Gold	69,030.
11	5' 1"	"Classic Alexandra" Polished Ebony	53,320.
11	5' 1"	"Classic Alexandra" Pol. Mahogany	55,452.
11	5' 1"	"Classic Alexandra" Polished Walnut	55,986.
10	5' 5"	Ebony or Polished Ebony	52,516.
10	5' 5"	Walnut or Polished Walnut	55,554.
10	5' 5"	Mahogany or Polished Mahogany	55,024.
10	5' 5"	Cherry or Polished Cherry	55,290.
10	5' 5"	White or Polished White	55,140.
10	5' 5"	Polished Bubinga, Yew, Macassar Eby.	58,200.
10	5' 5"	Saxony Polished Pyramid Mahogany	68,780.
10	5' 5"	Saxony Polished Burl Walnut Inlay	69,444.
10	5' 5"	"President" Polished Ebony	60,368.
10	5' 5"	"President" Polished Mahogany	62,782.
10	5' 5"	"President" Polished Walnut	63,386.
10	5' 5"	"President" Polished Bubinga	66,404.
10	5' 5"	"Senator" French Walnut with Leather	65,856.
10	5' 5"	"Senator" Jacaranda Rosewd w/Leather	70,246.
10	5' 5"	Louis XV Ebony or Polished Ebony	63,110.
10	5' 5"	Louis XV Mahogany or Pol. Mahogany	60,050.
10	5' 5"	Louis XV Walnut or Polished Walnut	66,268.
10	5' 5"	"Kaiser Wilhelm II" Polished Ebony	63,662.
10	5' 5"	"Kaiser Wilhelm II" Pol. Mahogany	66,206.
10	5' 5"	"Kaiser Wilhelm II" Polished Walnut	66,844.

Model	Size	Style and Finish	Price*
10	5' 5"	"Kaiser Wilhelm II" Polished Cherry	66,524.
10	5' 5"	"Ambassador" East Indian Rosewood	74,088.
10	5' 5"	"Ambassador" Walnut	68,600.
10	5' 5"	"Nicolas II" Walnut with Burl Inlay	74,088.
10	5' 5"	Louis XVI Rococo White with Gold	79,576.
10	5' 5"	"Classic Alexandra" Polished Ebony	61,466.
10	5' 5"	"Classic Alexandra" Pol. Mahogany	63,924.
10	5' 5"	"Classic Alexandra" Polished Walnut	64,538.
6	6' 3"	Ebony or Polished Ebony	56,690.
6	6' 3"	Walnut or Polished Walnut	59,972.
6	6' 3"	Mahogany or Polished Mahogany	59,400.
6	6' 3"	Cherry or Polished Cherry	59,682.
6	6' 3"	White or Polished White	59,524.
6	6' 3"	Polished Bubinga, Yew, Macassar Eby.	62,828.
6	6' 3"	Saxony Polished Pyramid Mahogany	74,250.
6	6' 3"	Saxony Polished Burl Walnut Inlay	74,964.
6	6' 3"	"President" Polished Ebony	65,168.
6	6' 3"	"President" Polished Mahogany	67,774.
6	6' 3"	"President" Polished Walnut	68,426.
6	6' 3"	"President" Polished Bubinga	71,686.
6	6' 3"	"Senator" French Walnut with Leather	71,092.
6	6' 3"	"Senator" Jacaranda Rosewd w/Leather	75,830.
6	6' 3"	Louis XV Ebony or Polished Ebony	68,130.
6	6' 3"	Louis XV Mahogany or Pol. Mahogany	67,462.
6	6' 3"	Louis XV Walnut or Polished Walnut	71,538.
6	6' 3"	"Kaiser Wilhelm II" Polished Ebony	68,724.
6	6' 3"	"Kaiser Wilhelm II" Pol. Mahogany	71,470.
6	6' 3"	"Kaiser Wilhelm II" Polished Walnut	72,158.
6	6' 3"	"Kaiser Wilhelm II" Polished Cherry	71,816.
6	6' 3"	"Ambassador" East Indian Rosewood	79,978.
6	6' 3"	"Ambassador" Walnut	74,054.
6	6' 3"	"Nicolas II" Walnut with Burl Inlay	79,978.
6	6' 3"	Louis XVI Rococo White with Gold	85,904.
6	6' 3"	"Classic Alexandra" Polished Ebony	66,354.
6	6' 3"	"Classic Alexandra" Pol. Mahogany	69,008.
6	6' 3"	"Classic Alexandra" Polished Walnut	69,670.
6	6' 3"	"Jubilee" Ebony and Polished Ebony	61,890.

***For explanation of terms and prices, please see pages 20–25.**

Model	Size	Style and Finish	Price*

Blüthner (continued)

6	6' 3"	"Jubilee" Louis XV Polished Ebony	73,330.
6	6' 3"	"Jubilee" Louis XV Polished Mahogany	72,662.
6	6' 3"	"Jubilee" Louis XV Polished Walnut	76,738.
4	6' 10"	Ebony or Polished Ebony	64,536.
4	6' 10"	Walnut or Polished Walnut	68,270.
4	6' 10"	Mahogany or Polished Mahogany	67,620.
4	6' 10"	Cherry or Polished Cherry	67,946.
4	6' 10"	White or Polished White	67,762.
4	6' 10"	Polished Bubinga, Yew, Macassar Eby.	71,524.
4	6' 10"	Saxony Polished Pyramid Mahogany	84,528.
4	6' 10"	Saxony Polished Burl Walnut Inlay	85,338.
4	6' 10"	"President" Polished Ebony	74,188.
4	6' 10"	"President" Polished Mahogany	77,152.
4	6' 10"	"President" Polished Walnut	77,896.
4	6' 10"	"President" Polished Bubinga	81,604.
4	6' 10"	"Kaiser Wilhelm II" Polished Ebony	78,234.
4	6' 10"	"Kaiser Wilhelm II" Pol. Mahogany	81,362.
4	6' 10"	"Kaiser Wilhelm II" Polished Walnut	82,144.
4	6' 10"	"Kaiser Wilhelm II" Polished Cherry	81,754.
4	6' 10"	"Ambassador" East Indian Rosewood	91,048.
4	6' 10"	"Ambassador" Walnut	84,302.
4	6' 10"	"Classic Alexandra" Polished Ebony	75,536.
4	6' 10"	"Classic Alexandra" Pol. Mahogany	78,556.
4	6' 10"	"Classic Alexandra" Polished Walnut	79,314.
4	6' 10"	*"Left-handed" Piano, Polished Ebony*	74,226.
2	7' 8"	Ebony or Polished Ebony	72,128.
2	7' 8"	Walnut or Polished Walnut	76,304.
2	7' 8"	Mahogany or Polished Mahogany	75,576.
2	7' 8"	Cherry or Polished Cherry	75,938.
2	7' 8"	White or Polished White	75,734.
2	7' 8"	Polished Bubinga, Yew, Macassar Eby.	79,938.
2	7' 8"	Saxony Polished Pyramid Mahogany	94,472.
2	7' 8"	Saxony Polished Burl Walnut Inlay	95,378.
2	7' 8"	"President" Polished Ebony	82,916.
2	7' 8"	"President" Polished Mahogany	86,232.

Model	Size	Style and Finish	Price*
2	7' 8"	"President" Polished Walnut	87,062.
2	7' 8"	"President" Polished Bubinga	91,206.
2	7' 8"	"Kaiser Wilhelm II" Polished Ebony	87,438.
2	7' 8"	"Kaiser Wilhelm II" Pol. Mahogany	90,934.
2	7' 8"	"Kaiser Wilhelm II" Polished Walnut	91,808.
2	7' 8"	"Kaiser Wilhelm II" Polished Cherry	90,814.
2	7' 8"	"Ambassador" East Indian Rosewood	101,758.
2	7' 8"	"Ambassador" Walnut	94,222.
1	9' 2"	Ebony or Polished Ebony	86,048.
1	9' 2"	Walnut or Polished Walnut	91,028.
1	9' 2"	Mahogany or Polished Mahogany	90,160.
1	9' 2"	Cherry or Polished Cherry	90,596.
1	9' 2"	White or Polished White	90,350.
1	9' 2"	"President" Polished Ebony	98,916.
1	9' 2"	"President" Polished Mahogany	102,872.
1	9' 2"	"President" Polished Walnut	103,862.
1	9' 2"	"President" Polished Bubinga	108,808.
1	9' 2"	*"Left-handed" Piano, Polished Ebony*	98,968.
—	—	*Jubilee Edition Plate, any model, add'l*	5,200.

Bösendorfer

Prices do not include bench.

Verticals			
130CL	52"	Polished Ebony	41,778.
130CL	52"	Open-pore Walnut and Polished Walnut	43,978.
130CL	52"	Open-pore Mahogany and Pol. Mahog.	43,978.
130CL	52"	Satin and Polished Pommelé Mahogany	43,978.
130CL	52"	Satin and Polished Pyramid Mahogany	46,178.
130CL	52"	Bubinga and Polished Bubinga	43,978.
130CL	52"	Amboyna and Polished Amboyna	43,978.
130CL	52"	Satin and Polished Bird's-Eye Maple	46,178.
130CL	52"	Open-pore Rio Rosewood	46,178.
130CL	52"	White and Polished White	43,978.
Grands			
170CS	5' 8"	"Conservatory" Semi-gloss Ebony	57,178.
170	5' 8"	Polished Ebony	79,178.

***For explanation of terms and prices, please see pages 20–25.**

Model	Size	Style and Finish	Price*

Bösendorfer (continued)

170	5' 8"	Open-pore Walnut and Polished Walnut	83,578.
170	5' 8"	Open-pore Mahogany and Pol. Mahog.	83,578.
170	5' 8"	Satin and Polished Pommelé Mahogany	83,578.
170	5' 8"	Satin and Polished Pyramid Mahogany	88,858.
170	5' 8"	Bubinga and Polished Bubinga	83,578.
170	5' 8"	Amboyna and Polished Amboyna	88,858.
170	5' 8"	Satin and Polished Bird's-Eye Maple	88,858.
170	5' 8"	Open-pore Rio Rosewood	88,858.
170	5' 8"	White and Polished White	83,578.
170	5' 8"	"Johann Strauss" Polished Ebony	84,678.
170	5' 8"	"Franz Schubert" Polished Ebony	84,678.
170	5' 8"	"Franz Schubert" Polished Cherry	96,778.
170	5' 8"	"Senator," any finish	92,378.
170	5' 8"	"Chopin," any finish	114,378.
200CS	6' 7"	"Conservatory" Semi-gloss Ebony	61,578.
200	6' 7"	Polished Ebony	92,378.
200	6' 7"	Open-pore Walnut and Polished Walnut	100,298.
200	6' 7"	Open-pore Mahogany and Pol. Mahog.	100,298.
200	6' 7"	Satin and Polished Pommelé Mahogany	100,298.
200	6' 7"	Satin and Polished Pyramid Mahogany	105,138.
200	6' 7"	Bubinga and Polished Bubinga	100,298.
200	6' 7"	Amboyna and Polished Amboyna	105,138.
200	6' 7"	Satin and Polished Bird's-Eye Maple	105,138.
200	6' 7"	Open-pore Rio Rosewood	105,138.
200	6' 7"	White and Polished White	100,298.
200	6' 7"	"Johann Strauss" Polished Ebony	97,878.
200	6' 7"	"Franz Schubert" Polished Ebony	97,878.
200	6' 7"	"Franz Schubert" Polished Cherry	109,978.
200	6' 7"	"Senator," any finish	105,578.
200	6' 7"	"Chopin," any finish	127,578.
214CS	7'	"Conservatory" Semi-gloss Ebony	68,178.
214	7'	Polished Ebony	107,778.
214	7'	Open-pore Walnut and Polished Walnut	114,378.
214	7'	Open-pore Mahogany and Pol. Mahog.	114,378.
214	7'	Satin and Polished Pommelé Mahogany	114,378.

Model	Size	Style and Finish	Price*
214	7'	Satin and Polished Pyramid Mahogany	118,338.
214	7'	Bubinga and Polished Bubinga	114,378.
214	7'	Amboyna and Polished Amboyna	118,338.
214	7'	Satin and Polished Bird's-Eye Maple	118,338.
214	7'	Open-pore Rio Rosewood	118,338.
214	7'	White and Polished White	114,378.
214	7'	"Johann Strauss" Polished Ebony	113,278.
214	7'	"Franz Schubert" Polished Ebony	113,278.
214	7'	"Franz Schubert" Polished Cherry	125,378.
214	7'	"Senator," any finish	120,978.
214	7'	"Chopin," any finish	142,978.
225	7' 4"	Polished Ebony	114,378.
225	7' 4"	Open-pore Walnut and Polished Walnut	124,058.
225	7' 4"	Open-pore Mahogany and Pol. Mahog.	124,058.
225	7' 4"	Satin and Polished Pommelé Mahogany	124,058.
225	7' 4"	Satin and Polished Pyramid Mahogany	129,338.
225	7' 4"	Bubinga and Polished Bubinga	124,058.
225	7' 4"	Amboyna and Polished Amboyna	129,338.
225	7' 4"	Satin and Polished Bird's-Eye Maple	129,338.
225	7' 4"	Open-pore Rio Rosewood	129,338.
225	7' 4"	White and Polished White	124,058.
225	7' 4"	"Johann Strauss" Polished Ebony	119,878.
225	7' 4"	"Franz Schubert" Polished Ebony	119,878.
225	7' 4"	"Franz Schubert" Polished Cherry	129,778.
225	7' 4"	"Senator," any finish	125,378.
225	7' 4"	"Chopin," any finish	147,378.
225	7' 4"	"Hollein" Red with 24 Karat Gold	145,178.
275	9'	Polished Ebony	145,178.
275	9'	Open-pore Walnut and Polished Walnut	155,738.
275	9'	Open-pore Mahogany and Pol. Mahog.	155,738.
275	9'	Satin and Polished Pommelé Mahogany	155,738.
275	9'	Satin and Polished Pyramid Mahogany	161,898.
275	9'	Bubinga and Polished Bubinga	155,738.
275	9'	Amboyna and Polished Amboyna	161,898.
275	9'	Satin and Polished Bird's-Eye Maple	161,898.
275	9'	Open-pore Rio Rosewood	161,898.
275	9'	White and Polished White	155,738.

***For explanation of terms and prices, please see pages 20–25.**

Model	Size	Style and Finish	Price*

Bösendorfer (continued)

Model	Size	Style and Finish	Price*
275	9'	"Johann Strauss" Polished Ebony	153,978.
275	9'	"Franz Schubert" Polished Ebony	153,978.
275	9'	"Franz Schubert" Polished Cherry	162,778.
275	9'	"Senator," any finish	158,378.
275	9'	"Chopin," any finish	180,378.
280	9' 2"	Polished Ebony	153,978.
280	9' 2"	Open-pore Walnut and Polished Walnut	164,538.
280	9' 2"	Open-pore Mahogany and Pol. Mahog.	164,538.
280	9' 2"	Satin and Polished Pommelé Mahogany	164,538.
280	9' 2"	Satin and Polished Pyramid Mahogany	170,698.
280	9' 2"	Bubinga and Polished Bubinga	164,538.
280	9' 2"	Amboyna and Polished Amboyna	170,698.
280	9' 2"	Satin and Polished Bird's-Eye Maple	170,698.
280	9' 2"	Open-pore Rio Rosewood	170,698.
280	9' 2"	White and Polished White	164,538.
280	9' 2"	"Johann Strauss" Polished Ebony	162,778.
280	9' 2"	"Franz Schubert" Polished Ebony	162,778.
280	9' 2"	"Franz Schubert" Polished Cherry	171,578.
280	9' 2"	"Senator," any finish	167,178.
280	9' 2"	"Chopin," any finish	189,178.
290	9' 6"	Polished Ebony	175,978.
290	9' 6"	Open-pore Walnut and Polished Walnut	186,978.
290	9' 6"	Open-pore Mahogany and Pol. Mahog.	186,978.
290	9' 6"	Satin and Polished Pommelé Mahogany	186,978.
290	9' 6"	Satin and Polished Pyramid Mahogany	193,578.
290	9' 6"	Bubinga and Polished Bubinga	186,978.
290	9' 6"	Amboyna and Polished Amboyna	193,578.
290	9' 6"	Satin and Polished Bird's-Eye Maple	193,578.
290	9' 6"	Open-pore Rio Rosewood	193,578.
290	9' 6"	White and Polished White	186,978.
290	9' 6"	"Johann Strauss" Polished Ebony	182,578.
290	9' 6"	"Franz Schubert" Polished Ebony	182,578.
290	9' 6"	"Franz Schubert" Polished Cherry	193,578.
290	9' 6"	"Senator," any finish	189,178.
290	9' 6"	"Chopin," any finish	213,378.

Model	Size	Style and Finish	Price*
290	9' 6"	"Hollein" Red with 24 Karat Gold	219,780.
all models		"Chippendale," any finish	on request
all models		"Louis XV," any finish	on request
all models		"Baroque," any finish	on request

Boston

Verticals			
UP-118C	45"	Continental Polished Ebony	7,960.
UP-118C	45"	Continental Polished Walnut	8,680.
UP-118C	45"	Continental Polished Mahogany	8,680.
UP-118E	46"	Polished Ebony	8,460.
UP-118E	46"	Walnut	9,440.
UP-118E	46"	Polished Walnut	9,640.
UP-118E	46"	Polished Mahogany	9,640.
UP-118E	46"	Polished White	9,440.
UP-118A	46"	Aniegre	11,780.
UP-118S	46"	Open-Pore Honey Oak	6,700.
UP-118S	46"	Open-Pore Black Oak	6,700.
UP-118S	46"	Open-Pore Red Oak	6,700.
UP-118S	46"	Mahogany	7,400.
UP-118T	46"	Florentine Mahogany	10,780.
UP-118P	46"	Berkshire Cherry	10,780.
UP-125E	49"	Polished Ebony	9,540.
UP-125E	49"	Polished Mahogany	11,000.
UP-126E	50"	Polished Ebony	10,900.
UP-126E	50"	Polished Mahogany	12,580.
UP-132E	52"	Polished Ebony	11,540.
Grands			
GP-156	5' 1"	Ebony and Polished Ebony	15,720.
GP-163	5' 4"	Ebony	18,880.
GP-163	5' 4"	Polished Ebony	19,300.
GP-163	5' 4"	Mahogany	20,560.
GP-163	5' 4"	Polished Mahogany	21,040.
GP-163	5' 4"	Walnut	20,760.
GP-163	5' 4"	Polished Walnut	21,280.
GP-163	5' 4"	Polished White	19,840.

***For explanation of terms and prices, please see pages 20–25.**

Model	Size	Style and Finish	Price*

Boston (continued)

GP-163	5' 4"	Polished Ivory	19,840.
GP-178	5' 10"	Ebony	21,780.
GP-178	5' 10"	Polished Ebony	22,240.
GP-178	5' 10"	Mahogany	23,200.
GP-178	5' 10"	Polished Mahogany	23,700.
GP-178	5' 10"	Walnut	23,460.
GP-178	5' 10"	Polished Walnut	24,160.
GP-178	5' 10"	Polished White	22,720.
GP-178	5' 10"	Polished Ivory	22,720.
GP-193	6' 4"	Ebony	27,580.
GP-193	6' 4"	Polished Ebony	28,280.
GP-193	6' 4"	Walnut	30,720.
GP-193	6' 4"	Polished Mahogany	30,940.
GP-193	6' 4"	Polished White	29,760.
GP-218	7' 2"	Ebony	35,020.
GP-218	7' 2"	Polished Ebony	35,920.

Brentwood—see "Westbrook"

Broadwood, John, & Sons

Prices are FOB England and do not include duty, freight, and other costs of importing. Oak, ash, and cherry are available at the same price as mahogany. Polished white is available at the same price as polished ebony.

Verticals

St. James	44"	Polished Ebony	8,085.
St. James	44"	Mahogany	6,900.
St. James	44"	Polished Mahogany	8,085.
St. James	44"	Walnut	6,900.
St. James	44"	Polished Walnut	8,085.
Berwick	47"	Polished Ebony	9,465.
Berwick	47"	Mahogany	8,100.
Berwick	47"	Polished Mahogany	9,465.
Berwick	47"	Walnut	8,100.
Berwick	47"	Polished Walnut	9,465.

Model	Size	Style and Finish	Price*
Imperial	47"	Mahogany	9,420.
Imperial	47"	Polished Mahogany	10,590.
Stratford	50"	Polished Ebony	13,575.
Stratford	50"	Mahogany	12,510.
Stratford	50"	Polished Mahogany	13,575.
Stratford	50"	Walnut	12,510.
Stratford	50"	Polished Walnut	13,575.
Grands			
Boudoir	6' 1"	Polished Ebony	41,970.

Charles R. Walter — see "Walter, Charles R."

Chickering

Grands			
CH162	5' 4"	Ebony and Polished Ebony	14,190.
CH162	5' 4"	French Provincial Cherry	17,190.
CH162	5' 4"	Queen Anne Cherry	17,190.
CH162	5' 4"	Polished White	14,190.
CH176	5' 9"	Ebony and Polished Ebony	16,390.
CH176	5' 9"	French Provincial Cherry	19,790.
CH176	5' 9"	Chippendale Cherry	19,790.
CH176	5' 9"	Louis XV Polished Mahogany	19,790.
CH176	5' 9"	Polished Ivory	16,390.
CH189	5' 9"	Ebony and Polished Ebony	19,190.
CH189	5' 9"	Louis XV Polished Mahogany	23,190.

Conn

Verticals			
C433	43"	French Cherry	2,790.
C434	43"	French Oak	2,790.
C435	43"	Oak	2,790.
C436	43"	Cherry	2,790.

***For explanation of terms and prices, please see pages 20–25.**

Model	Size	Style and Finish	Price*

Essex

Verticals

EUP-107C	42"	Continental Polished Ebony	5,190.
EUP-111E	44"	European Polished Ebony	5,750.
EUP-111E	44"	European Polished Mahogany	5,890.
EUP-111F	44"	French Provincial Cherry	6,270.
EUP-111M	44"	Modern Walnut	5,990.
EUP-111R	44"	English Regency Mahogany	5,830.
EUP-111T	44"	Ash	5,870.

Grands

EGP-161	5' 3"	Ebony	14,060.
EGP-161	5' 3"	Polished Ebony	13,790.
EGP-161	5' 3"	Mahogany	15,180.
EGP-161	5' 3"	Polished Mahogany	14,900.
EGP-161	5' 3"	Walnut	15,580.
EGP-161	5' 3"	Cherry	15,820.
EGP-161	5' 3"	Oak	15,500.
EGP-161	5' 3"	Polished White	13,960.
EGP-161	5' 3"	Polished Ivory	13,960.
EGP-183	6'	Polished Ebony	17,840.

Estonia

Prices for 6' 3" and 9' models include Jansen adjustable artist bench. Prices for 5' 6" models do not include bench.

Grands

168	5' 6"	Ebony and Polished Ebony	20,375.
168	5' 6"	Mahogany and Polished Mahogany	22,020.
168	5' 6"	Bubinga and Polished Bubinga	22,020.
168	5' 6"	Walnut and Polished Walnut	22,020.
168	5' 6"	*White and Polished White*	22,020.
190	6' 3"	Ebony and Polished Ebony	25,650.
190	6' 3"	Mahogany and Polished Mahogany	28,210.
190	6' 3"	Bubinga and Polished Bubinga	28,210.
190	6' 3"	Walnut and Polished Walnut	28,210.
190	6' 3"	*White and Polished White*	28,210.

Model	Size	Style and Finish	Price*
190	6' 3"	*Chippendale Ebony and Polished Ebony*	26,575.
190	6' 3"	*Chippendale White and Polished White*	29,230.
273	9'	Ebony and Polished Ebony	47,150.
273	9'	*White and Polished White*	51,870.

Eterna

Verticals			
ERC 10	44"	Continental Polished Ebony	3,598.

Everett

Verticals			
EV-112	44"	Continental Polished Ebony	2,580.
EV-112	44"	Continental Polished Mahogany	2,700.
EV-113	45"	Polished Ebony	2,780.
EV-113	45"	Polished Mahogany	2,900.
Grands			
EV-152	5'	Polished Ebony	7,780.
EV-152	5'	Polished Mahogany	8,380.
EV-152	5'	Polished Walnut	8,580.
EV-152	5'	Polished White	8,380.
EV-165	5' 5"	Polished Ebony	8,780.
EV-165	5' 5"	Polished Mahogany	9,380.
EV-165	5' 5"	Polished Walnut	9,580.
EV-185	6' 1"	Polished Ebony	10,580.
EV-185	6' 1"	Polished Mahogany	11,180.
EV-185	6' 1"	Polished Walnut	11,380.

***For explanation of terms and prices, please see pages 20–25.**

Fazioli

Fazioli is willing to make custom-designed cases with exotic veneers, marquetry, and other embellishments. Prices on request to Fazioli.

Grands

Model	Size	Style and Finish	Price*
F156	5' 2"	Ebony and Polished Ebony	73,700.
F156	5' 2"	Walnut	76,600.
F156	5' 2"	Polished Walnut	79,100.
F156	5' 2"	Polished Pyramid Mahogany	81,600.
F156	5' 2"	Cherry	76,600.
F156	5' 2"	Polished Cherry	79,100.
F183	6'	Ebony and Polished Ebony	82,000.
F183	6'	Walnut	85,900.
F183	6'	Polished Walnut	88,200.
F183	6'	Polished Pyramid Mahogany	91,300.
F183	6'	Cherry	85,900.
F183	6'	Polished Cherry	88,200.
F212	6' 11"	Ebony and Polished Ebony	92,600.
F212	6' 11"	Walnut	96,600.
F212	6' 11"	Polished Walnut	99,300.
F212	6' 11"	Polished Pyramid Mahogany	102,700.
F212	6' 11"	Cherry	96,600.
F212	6' 11"	Polished Cherry	99,300.
F228	7' 6"	Ebony and Polished Ebony	104,000.
F228	7' 6"	Walnut	108,300.
F228	7' 6"	Polished Walnut	110,800.
F228	7' 6"	Polished Pyramid Mahogany	116,200.
F228	7' 6"	Cherry	108,300.
F228	7' 6"	Polished Cherry	110,800.
F278	9' 2"	Ebony and Polished Ebony	133,600.
F278	9' 2"	Walnut	139,200.
F278	9' 2"	Polished Walnut	143,500.
F278	9' 2"	Polished Pyramid Mahogany	148,400.
F278	9' 2"	Cherry	139,200.
F278	9' 2"	Polished Cherry	143,500.
F308	10' 2"	Ebony and Polished Ebony	174,000.
F308	10' 2"	Walnut	181,600.

Model	Size	Style and Finish	Price*
F308	10' 2"	Polished Walnut	184,000.
F308	10' 2"	Polished Pyramid Mahogany	189,600.
F308	10' 2"	Cherry	181,600.
F308	10' 2"	Polished Cherry	184,000.
All models		*Fourth Pedal, add'l*	6,200.
All models		*Third and Fourth Pedals (set), add'l*	7,700.
All models		*Magnetic Balanced Action, add'l*	8,500.

Feurich

Prices do not include bench.

Verticals

F 116	45-1/2"	Polished Ebony	10,994.
F 116	45-1/2"	Oak	10,672.
F 116	45-1/2"	Walnut	10,672.
F 116	45-1/2"	Beech	10,672.
F 116	45-1/2"	Tola	10,828.
F 117 SL	46-1/2"	Polished Ebony	9,490.
F 118	46-1/2"	Polished Ebony	12,302.
F 118	46-1/2"	Oak	12,073.
F 118	46-1/2"	Walnut	12,073.
F 118	46-1/2"	Polished Walnut	13,382.
F 118	46-1/2"	Polished Mahogany	13,382.
F 118	46-1/2"	Beech	12,073.
F 118	46-1/2"	Euoprean Cherry	12,400.
F 118	46-1/2"	Polished European Cherry	13,709.
F 118	46-1/2"	Plum	12,842.
F 118	46-1/2"	Swiss Pearwood	12,727.
F 118	46-1/2"	Platane	12,509.
F 118	46-1/2"	Appel-birch	12,469.
F 118	46-1/2"	Yew	13,164.
F 118	46-1/2"	Polished White	12,790.
F 123	48-1/2"	Polished Ebony	14,208.
F 123	48-1/2"	Oak	14,104.
F 123	48-1/2"	Walnut	14,104.
F 123	48-1/2"	Polished Walnut	15,401.
F 123	48-1/2"	Polished Mahogany	15,401.

***For explanation of terms and prices, please see pages 20–25.**

Model	Size	Style and Finish	Price*

Feurich (continued)

F 123	48-1/2"	Beech	14,104.
F 123	48-1/2"	European Cherry	14,311.
F 123	48-1/2"	Polished European Cherry	15,723.
F 123	48-1/2"	Yew	15,183.
F 123	48-1/2"	Rio Palisander	15,764.
F 123	48-1/2"	Polished White	14,747.
F 123	48-1/2"	*Sostenuto System, add'l*	1,246.
Grands			
F 172	5' 8"	Polished Ebony	36,049.
F 172	5' 8"	Pommelé Mahogany	38,644.
F 172	5' 8"	Chippendale Walnut	40,956.
F 172	5' 8"	Altdeutschem Rim, Polished Ebony	41,135.
F 227	7' 5"	Polished Ebony	55,712.
F 227	7' 5"	Pommelé Mahogany	58,929.
F 227	7' 5"	Altdeutschem Rim, Polished Ebony	61,421.

Förster, August

Prices do not include bench.

Verticals			
116C	46"	Chippendale Polished Ebony	14,390.
116C	46"	Chippendale Walnut	15,160.
116C	46"	Chippendale Polished Mahogany	14,470.
116C	46"	Chippendale Polished White	14,760.
116E	46"	Polished Ebony	14,390.
116E	46"	Walnut	15,160.
116E	46"	Polished Mahogany	14,470.
116E	46"	Polished White	14,760.
125G	50"	Polished Ebony	15,590.
125G	50"	Walnut	16,420.
125G	50"	Polished Mahogany	15,650.
125G	50"	Polished White	15,960.
Grands			
170	5' 8"	Polished Ebony	30,440.
170	5' 8"	Polished Walnut	31,640.

Model	Size	Style and Finish	Price*
170	5' 8"	Polished Mahogany	30,500.
170	5' 8"	Polished White	31,910.
170	5' 8"	"Classic" Polished Ebony	34,230.
170	5' 8"	"Classic" Polished Walnut	39,230.
170	5' 8"	"Classic" Polished Mahogany	34,910.
170	5' 8"	Chippendale, *additional*	7,590.
170	5' 8"	Antique	on request
170	5' 8"	Rococo	on request
190	6' 4"	Polished Ebony	33,800.
190	6' 4"	Polished Walnut	35,060.
190	6' 4"	Polished Mahogany	33,930.
190	6' 4"	Polished White	35,270.
190	6' 4"	"Classic" Polished Ebony	37,600.
190	6' 4"	"Classic" Polished Walnut	42,650.
190	6' 4"	"Classic" Polished Mahogany	38,330.
190	6' 4"	Chippendale, *additional*	7,590.
190	6' 4"	Antique	on request
215	7' 2"	Polished Ebony	38,110.
275	9' 1"	Polished Ebony	77,110.

George Steck — see "Steck, George"

Grotrian

Prices do not include bench.

Verticals			
Caret	44"	Polished Ebony	19,000.
Caret	44"	Polished Walnut	20,000.
Caret	44"	Polished Mahogany	20,000.
Classic	49"	Polished Ebony	23,800.
Classic	49"	Polished Walnut	25,400.
Classic	49"	Polished Mahogany	25,400.
Concertino	52"	Polished Ebony	27,200.
Grands			
Chambre	5' 4"	Ebony	44,600.
Chambre	5' 4"	Polished Ebony	49,000.

***For explanation of terms and prices, please see pages 20–25.**

Model	Size	Style and Finish	Price*

Grotrian (continued)

Chambre	5' 4"	Polished Walnut	53,800.
Cabinet	6' 3"	Ebony	49,400.
Cabinet	6' 3"	Polished Ebony	54,000.
Cabinet	6' 3"	Polished Walnut	59,000.
Concert	7' 4"	Ebony	60,800.
Concert	7' 4"	Polished Ebony	65,000.
Concert Royale	9' 2"	Polished Ebony	75,400.

Haessler

Prices do not include bench.

Verticals

115 K	45"	Ebony and Polished Ebony	11,982.
115 K	45"	Waxed Alder	11,744.
115 K	45"	Beech	11,744.
115 K	45"	Ash	11,744.
115 K	45"	White and Polished White	12,522.
118 K	47"	Ebony and Polished Ebony	13,404.
118 K	47"	Ebony with Walnut Accent	14,504.
118 K	47"	Mahogany and Polished Mahogany	14,124.
118 K	47"	Walnut and Polished Walnut	14,124.
118 K	47"	Cherry and Polished Cherry	14,524.
118 K	47"	Cherry with Yew Inlay, Satin and Polish	15,324.
118 K	47"	Oak	12,664.
118 K	47"	White and Polished White	13,964.
118 KM	47"	Ebony and Polished Ebony	14,204.
118 KM	47"	White and Polished White	14,804.
118 CH	47"	Mahogany and Polished Mahogany	15,324.
118 CH	47"	Walnut and Polished Walnut	15,664.
124 K	49"	Ebony and Polished Ebony	14,364.
124 K	49"	Ebony with Walnut Accent	15,184.
124 K	49"	Mahogany and Polished Mahogany	15,564.
124 K	49"	Walnut and Polished Walnut	15,564.
124 K	49"	Cherry and Polished Cherry	16,024.
124 K	49"	Cherry with Yew Inlay, Satin and Polish	16,824.

Model	Size	Style and Finish	Price*
124 K	49"	White and Polished White	14,964.
124 KM	49"	Ebony and Polished Ebony	14,922.
124 KM	49"	White and Polished White	14,922.
132	52"	Ebony and Polished Ebony	20,220.
Grands			
175	5' 8"	Ebony and Polished Ebony	36,822.
175	5' 8"	Mahogany and Polished Mahogany	39,776.
175	5' 8"	Saxony Polished Pyramid Mahogany	49,722.
175	5' 8"	Walnut and Polished Walnut	40,160.
175	5' 8"	Saxony Polished Burl Walnut	50,198.
175	5' 8"	Cherry and Polished Cherry	39,968.
175	5' 8"	Polished Bubinga	42,072.
175	5' 8"	White and Polished White	38,664.
186	6' 1"	Ebony and Polished Ebony	41,486.
186	6' 1"	Mahogany and Polished Mahogany	44,814.
186	6' 1"	Saxony Polished Pyramid Mahogany	56,020.
186	6' 1"	Walnut and Polished Walnut	45,246.
186	6' 1"	Saxony Polished Burl Walnut	56,558.
186	6' 1"	Cherry and Polished Cherry	45,030.
186	6' 1"	Polished Bubinga	47,402.
186	6' 1"	White and Polished White	43,562.

Hallet, Davis & Co.

Verticals			
UP-108D	42"	Continental Polished Ebony	2,500.
UP-108D	42"	Continental Polished Mahogany	2,550.
UP-108D	42"	Continental Polished Brown Mahogany	2,550.
UP-108D	42"	Continental Polished Walnut	2,550.
UP-108D	42"	Continental Polished Cherry	2,550.
UP-108D	42"	Continental Polished White	2,550.
UP-108M2	42"	Chippendale Polished Mahogany	2,790.
UP-108M2	42"	Chippendale Polished Brown Mahogany	2,790.
UP-108M2	42"	Chippendale Polished Cherry	2,790.
UP-110P2	44"	French Fruitwood	3,100.
UP-110P2	44"	French Cherry	3,100.
UP-110P2	44"	French Walnut	3,100.

***For explanation of terms and prices, please see pages 20–25.**

Model	Size	Style and Finish	Price*

Hallet, Davis & Co. (continued)

UP-110P2	44"	French Brown Mahogany	3,100.
HS-450	45"	Walnut	3,190.
HS-452	45"	French Walnut	3,190.
UP-115M	46"	Polished Ebony	2,790.
UP-115M	46"	Polished Mahogany	2,840.
UP-115M	46"	Polished Brown Mahogany	2,840.
UP-115M	46"	Polished Walnut	2,840.
UP-115M	46"	Polished Cherry	2,840.
HB-115LS	46"	Deluxe Polished Ebony	2,990.
HB-115LS	46"	Deluxe Polished Mahogany	2,990.
HB-120LS	48"	Polished Ebony	3,390.
HB-120LS	48"	Polished Mahogany	3,390.
HU-120B	48"	Polished Mahogany	3,790.
HU-131HX	52"	Polished Walnut	5,680.
HU-132B	52"	Polished Mahogany	5,990.
Grands			
HDG-1480	4' 11"	"Modern" Polished Ebony	8,590.
HDG-1480	4' 11"	"Modern" Polished Mahogany	8,990.
HDG-1480	4' 11"	"Modern" Polished Walnut	8,990.
HDG-1481	4' 11"	"Classic" Polished Ebony	8,990.
HDG-1481	4' 11"	"Classic" Polished Mahogany	8,990.
HDG-1481	4' 11"	"Classic" Polished Walnut	8,990.
GP-159	5' 3"	"Parlor" Polished Ebony	8,590.
GP-159	5' 3"	"Parlor" Polished Mahogany	8,990.
GP-159	5' 3"	"Parlor" Polished Walnut	8,990.
GP-159	5' 3"	"Parlor" Polished Cherry	8,990.
GP-159	5' 3"	"Parlor" Polished White	8,990.
HDG-1580	5' 3"	"Modern" Polished Ebony	9,190.
HDG-1580	5' 3"	"Modern" Polished Mahogany	9,590.
HDG-1580	5' 3"	"Modern" Polished Walnut	9,590.
HDG-1680	5' 7"	"Modern" Polished Ebony	9,590.
HDG-1680	5' 7"	"Modern" Polished Mahogany	9,990.
HDG-1680	5' 7"	"Modern" Polished Walnut	9,990.

Model	Size	Style and Finish	Price*

Hoffmann, W.

Grand prices include artist bench; vertical prices include junior artist bench.

Verticals

H-120	47"	Polished Ebony	14,300.
H-120	47"	Oak	14,200.
H-120	47"	Mahogany	14,200.
H-120	47"	Polished Mahogany	15,240.
H-120	47"	Walnut	14,200.
H-120	47"	Polished Walnut	15,240.
H-120	47"	Cherry	14,200.
H-120	47"	Polished Cherry	15,240.
H-120	47"	Alder	14,000.
H-120	47"	Polished White	14,840.
H-124	49"	Polished Ebony	15,140.
H-124	49"	Oak	15,040.
H-124	49"	Mahogany	15,040.
H-124	49"	Polished Mahogany	16,200.
H-124	49"	Walnut	15,040.
H-124	49"	Polished Walnut	16,200.
H-124	49"	Cherry	15,040.
H-124	49"	Polished Cherry	16,200.
H-124	49"	Polished White	15,660.
H-125	50"	Polished Ebony	15,140.
H-125	50"	Oak	15,040.
H-125	50"	Mahogany	15,040.
H-125	50"	Polished Mahogany	16,200.
H-125	50"	Walnut	15,040.
H-125	50"	Polished Walnut	16,200.
H-125	50"	Cherry	15,040.
H-125	50"	Polished Cherry	16,200.
H-125	50"	Polished White	15,660.

Grands

H-158	5' 2"	Polished Ebony	30,840.
H-158	5' 2"	Polished Mahogany	32,120.
H-158	5' 2"	Polished White	32,800.
H-158	5' 2"	Chippendale Polished Mahogany	34,280.

***For explanation of terms and prices, please see pages 20–25.**

Model	Size	Style and Finish	Price*

Hoffmann, W. (continued)

H-170	5' 7"	Polished Ebony	32,940.
H-170	5' 7"	Polished Mahogany	34,540.
H-170	5' 7"	Polished White	35,800.
H-170	5' 7"	Chippendale Polished Mahogany	36,900.
H-190	6' 3"	Polished Ebony	37,240.

Hofmann & Scholz / Mecklenburg

Verticals

NP-121	48"	Polished Ebony	7,998.

Hyundai

Verticals

U-800	42"	Continental Polished Ebony	3,998.
U-800	42"	Continental Walnut	3,758.
U-800	42"	Continental Polished Walnut	4,300.
U-800	42"	Continental Polished Mahogany	4,300.
U-800	42"	Continental Polished Ivory	3,998.
U-824F	43"	French Walnut	4,998.
U-824F	43"	French Brown Oak	4,998.
U-824F	43"	French Cherry	4,998.
U-824M	43"	Mediterranean Brown Oak	4,998.
U-824M	43"	Mediterranean Walnut	4,998.
U-822	45"	Continental Polished Ebony	4,698.
U-822	45"	Continental Polished Mahogany	4,998.
U-852	46"	Ebony	5,598.
U-852	46"	Polished Ebony	5,598.
U-852	46"	Brown Oak	5,598.
U-852	46"	Walnut	5,198.
U-842	46"	Chippendale Polished Mahogany	5,598.
U-832	48"	Ebony	5,198.
U-832	48"	Polished Ebony	5,198.
U-832	48"	Walnut	5,398.
U-832	48"	Polished Walnut	5,398.

Model	Size	Style and Finish	Price*
U-832	48"	Brown Oak	5,398.
U-832	48"	Polished Brown Oak	5,398.
U-832	48"	Polished Mahogany	5,398.
U-837	52"	Ebony	5,598.
U-837	52"	Polished Ebony	5,698.
U-837	52"	Walnut	5,598.
U-837	52"	Polished Walnut	5,798.
U-837	52"	Polished Mahogany	5,798.
Grands			
G-50A	4' 7"	Ebony	9,898.
G-50A	4' 7"	Polished Ebony	9,998.
G-50A	4' 7"	Walnut	10,398.
G-50A	4' 7"	Polished Walnut	10,398.
G-50A	4' 7"	Polished Mahogany	10,398.
G-50A	4' 7"	Brown Oak	10,398.
G-50A	4' 7"	Polished Brown Oak	10,398.
G-50A	4' 7"	Polished Natural Oak	10,398.
G-50A	4' 7"	Cherry	10,398.
G-50A	4' 7"	Polished Ivory	10,198.
G-50A	4' 7"	Polished White	10,198.
G-50AF	4' 7"	Queen Anne Walnut	11,900.
G-50AF	4' 7"	Queen Anne Polished Walnut	11,900.
G-50AF	4' 7"	Queen Anne Brown Oak	11,900.
G-50AF	4' 7"	Queen Anne Polished Brown Oak	11,900.
G-50AF	4' 7"	Queen Anne Polished Mahogany	11,900.
G-50AF	4' 7"	Queen Anne Cherry	11,900.
G-50AF	4' 7"	Queen Anne Polished Ivory	11,900.
G-50AF	4' 7"	Queen Anne Polished White	11,900.
G-80A	5' 1"	Ebony	11,398.
G-80A	5' 1"	Polished Ebony	11,498.
G-80A	5' 1"	Walnut	11,898.
G-80A	5' 1"	Polished Walnut	11,898.
G-80A	5' 1"	Polished Natural Oak	11,898.
G-80A	5' 1"	Brown Oak	11,898.
G-80A	5' 1"	Polished Mahogany	11,898.
G-80A	5' 1"	Cherry	11,898.
G-80A	5' 1"	Polished Ivory	11,698.

***For explanation of terms and prices, please see pages 20–25.**

Model	Size	Style and Finish	Price*

Hyundai (continued)

G-80A	5' 1"	Polished White	11,698.
G-80AF	5' 1"	Queen Anne Polished Mahogany	14,098.
G-80B	5' 1"	Chippendale Polished Mahogany	14,098.
G-81	5' 9"	Chippendale Polished Mahogany	15,398.
G-82	5' 9"	Ebony	12,798.
G-82	5' 9"	Polished Ebony	12,898.
G-82	5' 9"	Walnut	13,298.
G-82	5' 9"	Polished Walnut	13,298.
G-82	5' 9"	Polished Natural Oak	13,298.
G-82	5' 9"	Brown Oak	13,298.
G-82	5' 9"	Polished Brown Oak	13,298.
G-82	5' 9"	Polished Mahogany	13,298.
G-82	5' 9"	Cherry	13,298.
G-82	5' 9"	Polished Ivory	13,098.
G-82	5' 9"	Polished White	13,098.
G-82AF	5' 9"	Queen Anne Polished Mahogany	15,398.
G-84	6' 1"	Ebony	13,498.
G-84	6' 1"	Polished Ebony	13,598.
G-84	6' 1"	Walnut	13,998.
G-84	6' 1"	Polished Walnut	13,998.
G-84	6' 1"	Brown Oak	13,998.
G-84	6' 1"	Polished Mahogany	13,998.
G-84	6' 1"	Polished Ivory	13,798.
G-84	6' 1"	Polished White	13,798.
G-85	6' 10"	Ebony	17,398.
G-85	6' 10"	Polished Ebony	17,398.

Irmler

Verticals

M113D	44"	Polished Ebony	6,010.
M113D	44"	Polished Walnut	6,220.
M113D	44"	Polished Mahogany	6,220.
M113D	44"	Cherry and Polished Cherry	6,220.
M113D	44"	Polished White	6,010.

Model	Size	Style and Finish	Price*
M118A	47"	Polished Ebony	6,410.
M118A	47"	Polished Walnut	6,640.
M118A	47"	Polished Mahogany	6,640.
M118A	47"	Cherry and Polished Cherry	6,640.
M118A	47"	Polished White	6,410.
M118CH	47"	Polished Ebony	7,280.
M118CH	47"	Polished Walnut	7,490.
M118CH	47"	Polished Mahogany	7,490.
M118CH	47"	Cherry and Polished Cherry	7,490.
M118CH	47"	Polished White	7,280.
M120A	48"	Polished Ebony	7,280.
M120A	48"	Polished Walnut	7,490.
M120A	48"	Polished Mahogany	7,490.
M120A	48"	Cherry and Polished Cherry	7,490.
M120A	48"	Polished White	7,280.
Grands			
F18E	5' 11"	Polished Ebony	25,110.
F18E	5' 11"	Polished Walnut	26,460.
F18E	5' 11"	Polished Mahogany	26,460.
F18E	5' 11"	Cherry and Polished Cherry	26,460.
F18E	5' 11"	Polished White	25,110.
F18E	5' 11"	Chippendale Polished Ebony	27,670.
F18E	5' 11"	Chippendale Polished Walnut	28,700.
F18E	5' 11"	Chippendale Polished Mahogany	28,700.
F18E	5' 11"	Chippendale Cherry and Pol. Cherry	28,700.
F18E	5' 11"	Chippendale Polished White	27,670.
F18E	5' 11"	"Classic" Polished Ebony	29,430.
F18E	5' 11"	"Classic" Polished Walnut	30,470.
F18E	5' 11"	"Classic" Polished Mahogany	30,470.
F18E	5' 11"	"Classic" Cherry and Polished Cherry	30,470.
F18E	5' 11"	"Classic" Polished White	29,430.

***For explanation of terms and prices, please see pages 20–25.**

Model	Size	Style and Finish	Price*

Kawai

Verticals

CX-10	44"	Polished Ebony	5,190.
506S	44-1/2"	Mahogany	3,790.
506S	44-1/2"	Oak	3,790.
606	44-1/2"	American Traditional Oak	4,390.
606	44-1/2"	French Renaissance Cherry	4,590.
606	44-1/2"	Queen Anne Classic Mahogany	4,690.
606	44-1/2"	Royal Queen Anne Cherry	5,990.
606	44-1/2"	Spanish Provincial Oak	5,890.
UST-7	46"	Ebony	6,690.
UST-7	46"	Oak	6,690.
UST-7	46"	Walnut	6,790.
UST-8	46"	Ebony	5,590.
UST-8	46"	Walnut	5,590.
UST-8	46"	Oak	5,590.
906-M	46-1/2"	Country Manor Oak	7,090.
906-T	46-1/2"	English Regency Mahogany	7,190.
906-F	46-1/2"	French Provincial Cherry	7,190.
K-25	48"	Polished Ebony	5,590.
K-30	48"	Polished Ebony	6,390.
K-30 ME	48"	"Millenium Edition" Polished Ebony	6,590.
K-30	48"	Mahogany	7,390.
K-30	48"	Polished Mahogany	7,590.
K-30	48"	Polished Snow White	6,790.
K-50	49"	Polished Ebony	7,790.
K-50 ME	49"	"Millenium Edition" Polished Ebony	8,290.
K-50	49"	Walnut	8,590.
K-50	49"	Polished Walnut	8,990.
K-50	49"	Polished Sapeli Mahogany	8,990.
K-60	52"	Polished Ebony	10,490.
K-80	52"	Polished Ebony	12,590.

Grands

GM-10	5'	Ebony	12,290.
GM-10	5'	Polished Ebony	12,390.
GM-10	5'	Polished Snow White	13,590.

Model	Size	Style and Finish	Price*
GE-20	5' 1"	Ebony	14,490.
GE-20	5' 1"	Polished Ebony	14,890.
GE-20	5' 1"	Walnut	16,390.
GE-20	5' 1"	Mahogany	16,190.
GE-20	5' 1"	Polished Mahogany	16,590.
GE-20	5' 1"	Polished Sapeli Mahogany	16,590.
GE-20	5' 1"	Polished Snow White	15,990.
GE-20	5' 1"	Polished Ivory	15,990.
GE-20F	5' 1"	French Provincial Polished Mahogany	17,990.
GE-30	5' 5"	Polished Ebony	16,590.
RX-1	5' 5"	Ebony	18,590.
RX-1	5' 5"	Polished Ebony	18,990.
RX-1	5' 5"	Walnut	20,370.
RX-1	5' 5"	Polished Walnut	20,990.
RX-1	5' 5"	Polished Sapeli Mahogany	20,590.
RX-1	5' 5"	Polished Snow White	19,790.
RX-2	5' 10"	Ebony	21,390.
RX-2	5' 10"	Polished Ebony	21,590.
RX-2	5' 10"	Walnut	23,190.
RX-2	5' 10"	Polished Walnut	24,390.
RX-2	5' 10"	Oak	22,190.
RX-2	5' 10"	Polished Sapeli Mahogany	23,390.
RX-2	5' 10"	Polished Rosewood	27,590.
RX-2	5' 10"	Polished Snow White	22,590.
RX-2F	5' 10"	French Provincial Polished Mahogany	27,390.
RX-3	6' 1"	Ebony	27,390.
RX-3	6' 1"	Polished Ebony	27,990.
RX-3	6' 1"	Walnut	29,990.
RX-3	6' 1"	Polished Sapeli Mahogany	30,590.
RX-3	6' 1"	Polished Snow White	28,990.
RX-5	6' 6"	Ebony	30,990.
RX-5	6' 6"	Polished Ebony	31,190.
RX-5	6' 6"	Polished Sapeli Mahogany	33,990.
RX-5	6' 6"	Polished Snow White	32,590.
RX-6	7'	Ebony	34,790.
RX-6	7'	Polished Ebony	34,990.
RX-7	7' 6"	Ebony	39,790.

***For explanation of terms and prices, please see pages 20–25.**

Model	Size	Style and Finish	Price*

Kawai (continued)

RX-7	7' 6"	Polished Ebony	40,190.
GS-100	9' 1"	Ebony	77,990.
GS-100	9' 1"	Polished Ebony	79,990.
EX	9' 1"	Polished Ebony	109,190.
EX-G	9' 1"	Polished Ebony	115,990.

Kemble

Verticals

Oxford	43"	Polished Ebony	7,710.
Oxford	43"	Mahogany	6,790.
Oxford	43"	Georgian Mahogany Lustre	7,710.
Oxford	43"	Polished Mahogany	7,710.
Oxford	43"	Polished Walnut	7,710.
Oxford	43"	Beech	7,710.
Traditional	45"	Polished Ebony with Burr Walnut	8,650.
Traditional	45"	Polished Mahogany	8,350.
Prestige	45"	Cherry with Yew Inlay	9,490.
Empire	45"	Empire Polished Mahogany	9,690.
Windsor	46-1/2"	Polished Ebony with Burr Walnut	8,950.
Windsor	46-1/2"	Georgian Mahogany Lustre	8,750.
Windsor	46-1/2"	Polished Mahogany	8,750.
K121Z	48"	Polished Ebony	9,590.
K121Z	48"	Georgian Mahogany Lustre	9,290.
K121Z	48"	Polished Mahogany	9,590.
K121Z	48"	Polished Walnut	9,590.
K131	52"	Polished Ebony	13,350.
K131	52"	Polished Mahogany	13,350.

Kingsburg

Verticals

109AB	43"	Continental Polished Ebony	3,885.
109AP	43"	Continental Polished Mahogany	3,975.
109AP	43"	Continental Polished Walnut	3,975.
109AYS	43"	Continental Cherry	3,975.

Model	Size	Style and Finish	Price*
109AYS	43"	Continental Oak	3,975.
109BBS	43"	Continental Polished Ebony w/Molding	4,185.
LF109ABF	43"	Continental Pol. Mahogany w/Molding	4,335.
LF109ABF	43"	Continental Polished Walnut w/Molding	4,335.
109BB	43"	Polished Ebony (straight leg)	4,185.
LF109BM	43"	Polished Mahogany (straight leg)	4,185.
LF109BM	43"	Polished Walnut (straight leg)	4,185.
LF109GB	43"	Polished Ebony (curved leg)	4,335.
LF109GM	43"	Polished Mahogany (curved leg)	4,485.
LF109GM	43"	Polished Walnut (curved leg)	4,485.
LF113G	44"	Queen Anne or Mediterranean Oak	5,340.
LF113G	44"	Queen Anne or Mediterranean Cherry	5,340.
LF113G	44"	Queen Anne or Mediterranean Walnut	5,340.
LM115GW	45"	Polished Ebony	4,455.
LM115GW	45"	Polished Mahogany	4,455.
LM115GW	45"	Walnut	4,635.
LM115GW	45"	Polished Walnut	4,455.
LM115GW	45"	Oak	4,635.
LM115GW	45"	Cherry	4,635.
LM116EBF	46"	Chippendale Polished Ebony	4,395.
LM116EMF	46"	Chippendale Polished Mahogany	4,485.
LM116EMF	46"	Chippendale Polished Walnut	4,485.
LM116HB/M	46"	Pol. Ebony w/Oak or Cherry Accents	4,395.
LM117CW	46"	Cherry	5,685.
LM117CW	46"	Oak	5,685.
LM117CW	46"	Walnut	5,685.
LM117GW	46"	Polished Ebony (curved leg)	4,785.
LM117GW	46"	Polished Mahogany (curved leg)	4,785.
LM117GW	46"	Polished Walnut (curved leg)	4,785.
LT122BB	48"	Polished Ebony	5,085.
LT122BB	48"	Polished Mahogany	5,085.
LT122BB	48"	Polished Walnut	5,085.
LT122JB	48"	Polished Ebony with Cherry Accents	7,485.
LT122KB	48"	Polished Ebony w/Burr Walnut Accents	8,175.
LT122GW	48"	Cherry	5,985.
LT122GW	48"	Walnut	5,985.
LT122GW	48"	Oak	5,985.

***For explanation of terms and prices, please see pages 20–25.**

Kingsburg (continued)

Model	Size	Style and Finish	Price*
Grands			
F158	5' 2"	Polished Ebony	14,085.
F158	5' 2"	Polished Mahogany	14,085.
F185	6' 1"	Polished Ebony	16,485.
F185	6' 1"	Polished Mahogany	16,485.

Knight, Alfred

Prices are FOB England and do not include duty, freight, and other costs of importing. Oak, ash, and cherry are available at the same price as mahogany. Polished white is available at the same price as polished ebony.

Model	Size	Style and Finish	Price*
Verticals			
K10 Slimline	44"	Polished Ebony	10,605.
K10 Slimline	44"	Mahogany	8,955.
K10 Slimline	44"	Polished Mahogany	10,605.
K10 Slimline	44"	Walnut	8,955.
K10 Slimline	44"	Polished Walnut	10,605.
K10 Slimline	44"	Teak	8,955.
K10 London	44"	Polished Ebony	11,760.
K10 London	44"	Mahogany	9,885.
K10 London	44"	Polished Mahogany	11,760.
K10 London	44"	Walnut	9,885.
K10 London	44"	Polished Walnut	11,760.
K10 School	44"	Mahogany	9,690.
K10 School	44"	Oak	9,690.
Savoy	48"	Polished Ebony	12,510.
Savoy	48"	Mahogany	11,175.
Savoy	48"	Polished Mahogany	12,510.
Savoy	48"	Walnut	11,175.
Savoy	48"	Polished Walnut	12,510.

Model	Size	Style and Finish	Price*

Kohler & Campbell

Verticals

KC 142	42-1/2"	Continental Polished Ebony	2,590.
KC 142	42-1/2"	Continental Cherry	2,690.
KC 142	42-1/2"	Continental Walnut	2,690.
KC 142	42-1/2"	Continental Mahogany	2,690.
KC 142	42-1/2"	Continental Oak	2,690.
KC 142	42-1/2"	Continental Polished Ivory	2,590.
KC 142	42-1/2"	Continental Polished White	2,590.
KC 144T	44"	Cherry	3,390.
KC 144T	44"	Mahogany	3,390.
KC 144M	44"	Mediterranean Brown Oak	3,290.
KC 144F	44"	French Provincial Brown Oak	3,390.
KC 144F	44"	French Provincial Cherry	3,390.
KC 145	45"	Polished Ebony	2,790.
KC 145	45"	Cherry	2,890.
KC 145	45"	Walnut	2,890.
KC 145	45"	Mahogany	2,890.
KC 145	45"	Oak	2,890.
KC 145	45"	Polished Ivory	2,790.
KC 145	45"	Polished White	2,790.
KC 118T	46-1/2"	Cherry	3,990.
KC 118T	46-1/2"	Mahogany	3,990.
KC 118M	46-1/2"	Mediterranean Brown Oak	3,790.
KC 118F	46-1/2"	French Provincial Brown Oak	3,990.
KC 118F	46-1/2"	French Provincial Cherry	3,990.
SKV-465S	46-1/2"	Ebony and Polished Ebony	4,390.
SKV-465S	46-1/2"	Walnut and Polished Walnut	4,590.
SKV-465S	46-1/2"	Mahogany and Polished Mahogany	4,590.
SKV-465S	46-1/2"	Oak and Polished Oak	4,590.
SKV-118FA	46-1/2"	French Polished Mahogany	5,190.
SKV-118FA	46-1/2"	French Polished Walnut	5,190.
KMV-47T	46-1/2"	"Millennium" Polished Cherry	5,190.
KMV-47T	46-1/2"	"Millennium" Polished Mahogany	5,190.
KMV-47F	46-1/2"	"Millennium" French Polished Cherry	5,190.
KC 121F	48"	Polished Ebony	3,990.

***For explanation of terms and prices, please see pages 20–25.**

Model	Size	Style and Finish	Price*

Kohler & Campbell (continued)

Model	Size	Style and Finish	Price*
KC 121F	48"	Polished Mahogany	4,190.
KC 121M	48"	Polished Ebony	3,890.
KC 121M	48"	Polished Mahogany	4,090.
KC 121M	48"	Polished White	4,090.
SKV-48S	48"	Ebony and Polished Ebony	4,590.
SKV-48S	48"	Walnut and Polished Walnut	4,790.
SKV-48S	48"	Polished Mahogany	4,790.
SKV-48S	48"	Oak and Polished Oak	4,790.
SKV-48S	48"	Polished Ivory	4,590.
SKV-48S	48"	Polished White	4,590.
KMV-48SD	48"	"Millennium" Polished Ebony	5,390.
KMV-48SD	48"	"Millennium" Polished Mahogany	5,590.
SKV-52S	52"	Ebony and Polished Ebony	5,390.
SKV-52S	52"	Walnut and Polished Walnut	5,590.
SKV-52S	52"	Polished Mahogany	5,590.
SKV-52S	52"	Polished White	5,390.
KMV-52MD	52"	"Millennium" Polished Ebony	5,990.
KMV-52MD	52"	"Millennium" Polished Mahogany	6,390.
Grands			
KIG 47	4' 7"	Polished Ebony	7,490.
KIG 47	4' 7"	Polished Mahogany	7,890.
SKG-400S	4' 7"	Ebony and Polished Ebony	9,140.
SKG-400S	4' 7"	Walnut and Polished Walnut	9,640.
SKG-400S	4' 7"	Mahogany and Polished Mahogany	9,640.
SKG-400S	4' 7"	Oak and Polished Oak	9,640.
SKG-400S	4' 7"	Cherry	9,640.
SKG-400S	4' 7"	Polished Ivory	9,140.
SKG-400S	4' 7"	Polished White	9,140.
SKG-400SKAF	4' 7"	French Provincial—all finishes (satin)	10,890.
SKG-400SKBF	4' 7"	French Provincial—all finishes (polish)	11,290.
SKG-500S	5' 1"	Ebony and Polished Ebony	10,700.
SKG-500S	5' 1"	Walnut and Polished Walnut	11,220.
SKG-500S	5' 1"	Mahogany and Polished Mahogany	11,220.
SKG-500S	5' 1"	Oak and Polished Oak	11,220.
SKG-500S	5' 1"	Cherry	11,220.

Model	Size	Style and Finish	Price*
SKG-500S	5' 1"	Polished Ivory	10,700.
SKG-500S	5' 1"	Polished White	10,700.
SKG-500SKAF	5' 1"	French Provincial—all finishes (polish)	12,410.
SKG-500SKBF	5' 1"	French Provincial—all finishes (polish)	12,840.
SKG-600S	5' 9"	Ebony and Polished Ebony	11,990.
SKG-600S	5' 9"	Walnut and Polished Walnut	12,500.
SKG-600S	5' 9"	Mahogany and Polished Mahogany	12,500.
SKG-600S	5' 9"	Oak and Polished Oak	12,500.
SKG-600S	5' 9"	Cherry	12,500.
SKG-600S	5' 9"	Polished Ivory	11,990.
SKG-600S	5' 9"	White and Polished White	11,990.
SKG-600SL	5' 9"	Empire Ebony and Polished Ebony	13,060.
SKG-600SL	5' 9"	Empire Mahogany and Pol. Mahogany	13,580.
SKG-600SL	5' 9"	Empire Ivory and Polished Ivory	13,060.
SKG-600SL	5' 9"	Empire White and Polished White	13,060.
KFM-600S	5' 9"	"Millennium" Ebony and Pol. Ebony	19,100.
KFM-600S	5' 9"	"Millennium" All other finishes	20,000.
SKG-650S	6' 1"	Ebony and Polished Ebony	12,840.
SKG-650S	6' 1"	Walnut and Polished Walnut	13,360.
SKG-650S	6' 1"	Mahogany and Polished Mahogany	13,360.
SKG-650S	6' 1"	Oak and Polished Oak	13,360.
SKG-650S	6' 1"	Cherry	13,360.
SKG-650SL	6' 1"	Empire Ebony and Polished Ebony	13,920.
SKG-650SL	6' 1"	Empire Mahogany and Pol. Mahogany	14,430.
KFM-650S	6' 1"	"Millennium" Ebony and Pol. Ebony	21,000.
KFM-650S	6' 1"	"Millennium" All other finishes	22,000.
KFM-650SL	6' 1"	"Millennium" Empire Satin/Pol. Ebony	21,900.
KFM-650SL	6' 1"	"Millennium" Empire Satin/Pol.Mahog.	22,900.
KFM-700S	6' 8"	"Millennium" Ebony and Pol. Ebony	24,000.
KFM-700S	6' 8"	"Millennium" All other finishes	25,000.
KFM-800S	7'	"Millennium" Ebony and Pol. Ebony	25,000.
KFM-850S	7' 4"	"Millennium" Ebony and Pol. Ebony	27,000.
KFM-900S	9' 1"	"Millennium" Ebony and Pol. Ebony	67,990.
KFM-900S	9' 1"	"Millennium" All other finishes	71,990.
KFM-900S	9' 1"	"Millennium" Bubinga	73,990.

***For explanation of terms and prices, please see pages 20–25.**

Model	Size	Style and Finish	Price*

Krakauer

Verticals

K443	43"	French Cherry	3,190.
K444	43"	French Oak	3,190.
K445	43"	Oak	3,190.
K446	43"	Cherry	3,190.
K110B	43"	Polished Ebony	3,190.
K110R	43"	Polished Mahogany	3,190.
K110T	43"	Polished Walnut	3,190.
K110W	43"	Polished White	3,190.
K120B	48"	Polished Ebony	3,390.
K120R	48"	Polished Mahogany	3,390.
K120T	48"	Polished Walnut	3,390.
K120W	48"	Polished White	3,390.
K122	48-3/4"	*Polished Ebony*	3,500.
K122	48-3/4"	*Polished Mahogany*	3,500.
K122	48-3/4"	*Polished Walnut*	3,500.
K122	48-3/4"	*Polished White*	3,500.
K125	50"	*Polished Ebony*	3,590.
K125	50"	*Polished Mahogany*	3,590.
K125	50"	*Polished Walnut*	3,590.
K125	50"	*Polished White*	3,590.

Mason & Hamlin

Verticals

50	50"	Polished Ebony	17,012.

Grands

A	5' 8"	Ebony	43,208.
A	5' 8"	Polished Ebony	46,206.
A	5' 8"	Mahogany	46,458.
A	5' 8"	Rosewood	51,566.
A	5' 8"	“Monticello” Polished Ebony	49,220.
A	5' 8"	“Monticello” Mahogany	49,458.
A	5' 8"	“Monticello” Rosewood	59,956.

Model	Size	Style and Finish	Price*
BB	7'	Ebony	56,498.
BB	7'	Polished Ebony	58,122.
BB	7'	Mahogany	58,498.
BB	7'	Rosewood	65,484.
BB	7'	“Monticello” Polished Ebony	60,898.
BB	7'	“Monticello” Mahogany	61,498.
BB	7'	“Monticello” Rosewood	75,472.

Mecklenburg — see “Hofmann & Scholz / Mecklenburg”

Niemeyer

Verticals

NI112	44"	Continental Polished Ebony	2,700.
NI112	44"	Continental Polished Mahogany	2,700.
NI112	44"	Continental Polished Walnut	2,700.
NI112	44"	Continental Polished White	2,700.
NI114	45"	Polished Ebony	2,900.
NI114	45"	Polished Mahogany	2,900.
NI121	48"	Polished Ebony	3,100.
NI121	48"	Polished Mahogany	3,100.

Niendorf

Prices do not include bench.

Grands

145	4' 9"	Polished Ebony	20,300.
145	4' 9"	Polished Mahogany	20,440.
145	4' 9"	Polished Walnut	20,890.
145	4' 9"	Chippendale Polished Ebony	21,230.
145	4' 9"	Chippendale Polished Mahogany	21,260.
145	4' 9"	Chippendale Polished Walnut	21,770.
182	6'	Polished Ebony	23,690.
182	6'	Polished Mahogany	24,870.
182	6'	Polished Walnut	24,760.

***For explanation of terms and prices, please see pages 20–25.**

Model	Size	Style and Finish	Price*

Nordiska

Model	Size	Style and Finish	Price*
Verticals			
112-F	44"	Continental Polished Ebony	2,780.
112-F	44"	Continental Polished Walnut	2,780.
112-F	44"	Continental Polished Mahogany	2,780.
116-C	46"	Polished Ebony	3,180.
116-C	46"	Polished Walnut	3,180.
116-C	46"	Polished Mahogany	3,180.
116-CB	46"	Chippendale Polished Ebony	3,580.
116-CB	46"	Chippendale Polished Walnut	3,580.
116-CB	46"	Chippendale Polished Mahogany	3,580.
118-S	46"	Demi-Chippendale Polished Ebony	3,380.
118-S	46"	Demi-Chippendale Polished Walnut	3,380.
118-S	46"	Demi-Chippendale Pol. Dark Walnut	3,380.
118-S	46"	Demi-Chippendale Polished Mahogany	3,380.
118-CH	47"	Polished Ebony	3,380.
118-CH	47"	Walnut	3,380.
120-C	48"	Polished Ebony	3,780.
120-C	48"	Polished Mahogany	3,780.
122-C	48"	Polished Ebony	3,780.
122-C	48"	Polished Mahogany	3,780.
Grands			
152-C	5'	Polished Ebony	7,600.
152-C	5'	Polished Mahogany	7,980.
152-C	5'	Walnut	7,980.
152-DC	5'	Demi-Chippendale Polished Ebony	8,350.
152-DC	5'	Demi-Chippendale Polished Mahogany	8,800.
165-CM	5' 5"	Polished Ebony	8,380.
165-CM	5' 5"	Polished Mahogany	8,700.
165-DC	5' 5"	Demi-Chippendale Polished Ebony	9,300.
165-DC	5' 5"	Demi-Chippendale Polished Mahogany	9,580.
165-R	5' 5"	Regency Polished Ebony	8,900.
165-R	5' 5"	Regency Polished Mahogany	9,180.
185-C	6' 1"	Polished Ebony	9,980.
185-DC	6' 1"	Demi-Chippendale Polished Ebony	10,900.
185-I	6' 1"	Imperial Polished Ebony	10,500.
185-I	6' 1"	Imperial Polished Mahogany	10,780.

Model	Size	Style and Finish	Price*

Pearl River

Verticals

UP-108D1	42-1/2"	Continental Polished Ebony	2,670.
UP-108D1	42-1/2"	Continental Polished Mahogany	2,720.
UP-108D1	42-1/2"	Continental Polished Walnut	2,720.
UP-108D1	42-1/2"	Continental Polished Cherry	2,720.
UP-108D1	42-1/2"	Continental Polished White	2,770.
UP-108M2	42-1/2"	Chippendale Polished Mahogany	2,850.
UP-108M2	42-1/2"	Chippendale Polished Walnut	2,850.
UP-108T2	42-1/2"	Euro-Studio Polished Ebony	2,900.
UP-108T2	42-1/2"	Euro-Studio Polished Mahogany	2,950.
UP-108T2	42-1/2"	Euro-Studio Polished Walnut	2,950.
UP-108T2	42-1/2"	Euro-Studio Polished White	2,990.
UP-110P2	43"	Country French Semi-Gloss Mahogany	3,460.
UP-110P2	43"	Country French Walnut	3,456.
UP-110P3	43"	French/Chippendale Polished Ebony	3,540.
UP-110P3	43"	French/Chippendale Pol. Mahogany	3,590.
UP-110P4	43"	Mahogany (sliding fallboard)	3,360.
UP-110P4	43"	Semi-Gloss Walnut (sliding fallboard)	3,360.
UP-110P5	43"	Mahogany (Boston fallboard)	3,460.
UP-110P5	43"	Semi-Gloss Walnut (Boston fallboard)	3,460.
UP-118M	47"	Polished Ebony	2,980.
UP-118M	47"	Polished Mahogany	3,030.
UP-118M	47"	Polished Walnut	3,030.
UP-118M	47"	Polished Cherry	3,030.
UP-118M	47"	Polished White	3,070.
UP-118M4	47"	Deluxe Polished Ebony	3,260.
UP-118M4	47"	Deluxe Polished Mahogany	3,310.
UP-118M4	47"	Deluxe Polished Walnut	3,310.
UP-125M1	49"	Polished Ebony (with Yamaha)	4,480.
UP-130M	51"	Polished Ebony	3,490.
UP-130M	51"	Polished Mahogany	3,530.
UP-130M	51"	Polished Walnut	3,530.
UP-130T2	51"	Euro Special Design Polished Ebony	4,970.
UP-130T2	51"	Euro Special Design Pol. Mahogany	5,020.

***For explanation of terms and prices, please see pages 20–25.**

Model	Size	Style and Finish	Price*

Pearl River (continued)

Grands

GP-142	4' 7"	Polished Ebony	8,140.
GP-142	4' 7"	Polished Mahogany	8,470.
GP-142	4' 7"	Polished Walnut	8,470.
GP-159	5' 3"	Polished Ebony	9,840.
GP-159	5' 3"	Polished Mahogany	10,170.
GP-159	5' 3"	Polished Walnut	10,170.
GP-159	5' 3"	Polished White	10,170.
GP-183	6'	Polished Ebony	13,730.
GP-188	6' 4"	Polished Ebony	16,200.
GP-188	6' 4"	Polished Mahogany	16,700.
GP-188	6' 4"	Polished Walnut	16,700.
GP-213	7'	Polished Ebony	17,980.
GP-213	7'	Polished Walnut	18,290.
GP-275	9'	Polished Ebony	on request

Petrof

Note: Prices below do not include bench. Add from $220 to $630 (most are under $400), depending on choice of bench.

Verticals

100-B	42"	"Barok" Polished Walnut	6,900.
100-B	42"	"Barok" Polished Flame Mahogany	6,900.
105-V	43"	"Futura" Polished Walnut	5,180.
105-V	43"	"Futura" Polished Mahogany	5,180.
115-I	45"	Demi-Chippendale Polished Ebony	6,500.
115-I	45"	Demi-Chippendale Polished Walnut	6,500.
115-I	45"	Demi-Chippendale Pol. Flame Mahog.	6,500.
115-I	45"	Demi-Chipp. With Designer Panel	6,700.
115-IC	45"	Chippendale Polished Ebony	6,780.
115-IC	45"	Chippendale Polished Walnut	6,780.
115-IC	45"	Chippendale Polished Flame Mahogany	6,780.
115-II	45"	Continental Polished Ebony	5,780.
115-II	45"	Continental Polished Walnut	5,780.
115-II	45"	Continental Polished Flame Mahogany	5,780.

Model	Size	Style and Finish	Price*
115-II	45"	Continental Polished Oak	5,780.
115-IID	45"	Polished Ebony	6,380.
115-IID	45"	Polished Walnut	6,380.
115-IID	45"	Polished Flame Mahogany	6,380.
115-V	45"	Polished Ebony	6,380.
115-V	45"	Polished Walnut	6,380.
115-V	45"	Polished Flame Mahogany	6,380.
115-VI	45"	Polished Ebony	6,180.
115-VI	45"	Polished Walnut	6,180.
115-VI	45"	Polished Flame Mahogany	6,180.
115-VII	45"	Polished Burl Walnut Veneer	6,380.
115	45"	*With Petrof/Renner action, add'l*	400.
125-III	50"	Polished Walnut	7,500.
125-III	50"	Polished Flame Mahogany	7,500.
125-III	50"	Polished Mahogany w/ Designer Panel	7,700.
125-IV	50"	Polished Ebony	7,580.
126	50"	"Elegante" Pol. Ebony w/ Walnut/Gold	8,100.
131	52"	Polished Ebony	10,180.
131	52"	Polished Walnut	10,180.
131	52"	Polished Flame Mahogany	10,180.
Grands			
V	5' 3"	Polished Ebony	19,500.
V	5' 3"	Polished Walnut	19,500.
V	5' 3"	Polished Flame Mahogany	19,500.
V	5' 3"	Demi-Chippendale Polished Ebony	21,800.
V	5' 3"	Demi-Chippendale Polished Walnut	21,800.
V	5' 3"	Demi-Chippendale Pol. Flame Mahog.	21,800.
IV	5' 8"	Polished Ebony	21,000.
IV	5' 8"	Polished Walnut	21,000.
IV	5' 8"	Polished Flame Mahogany	21,000.
IV	5' 8"	Demi-Chippendale Polished Ebony	23,000.
IV	5' 8"	Demi-Chippendale Polished Walnut	23,000.
IV	5' 8"	Demi-Chippendale Pol. Flame Mahog.	23,000.
IV C	5' 8"	Chippendale Polished Ebony	25,800.
IV C	5' 8"	Chippendale Polished Walnut	25,800.
IV C	5' 8"	Chippendale Polished Flame Mahogany	25,800.
III	6' 4"	Polished Ebony	25,000.

***For explanation of terms and prices, please see pages 20–25.**

Model	Size	Style and Finish	Price*

Petrof (continued)

III	6' 4"	Polished Walnut	25,000.
III	6' 4"	Polished Flame Mahogany	25,000.
III M	6' 4"	"Master" Polished Ebony	33,800.
II	7' 9"	"Symphony" Polished Ebony	37,800.
I	9' 3"	"Mondial" Polished Ebony	47,800.

PianoDisc

Prices for PianoDisc and QuietTime systems vary by piano manufacturer and installer. The following are suggested retail prices from PianoDisc. The usual dealer discounts may apply, especially as an incentive to purchase a piano.

228 CFX System, "factory-installed" or retrofitted:

Playback only	5,899.
Add for SymphonyPro Sound Module	1,299.
Add for TFT MIDI Record system	1,299.
Add for amplified speakers, pair	749.
Add for MX Music Expansion	1,299.
Add for MX Platinum	1,699.
Add for PianoAmp	459.
Add for PianoMute Rail	399.
Add for Home Theater Master Remote	399.

PianoCD System	4,999.
QuietTime GT0 System:	1,989.
MIDI Controller (TFT MIDI Strip and MIDI interface board)	1,849.

Pleyel

Verticals

PL 118	47"	Polished Ebony	12,320.
PL 118	47"	Polished Ebony with Cherry Decor	12,880.
PL 118	47"	Polished Mahogany	13,720.
PL 118	47"	Walnut with Marquetry	12,600.

Model	Size	Style and Finish	Price*
PL 124	49"	Polished Ebony	13,720.
PL 124	49"	Polished Ebony with Cherry	14,300.
PL 124	49"	Cherry/Walnut with Marquetry	14,000.
PL 131	51"	Polished Ebony	16,980.
PL 131	51"	*Add for Sostenuto*	990.
Grands			
PL 190	6' 3"	Polished Ebony	39,800.
PL 190	6' 3"	Cherry with Marquetry	49,000.
PL 190	6' 3"	Polished Mahogany	49,000.

Pramberger

Verticals			
JP-48	48"	Polished Ebony	7,390.
JP-48	48"	Bubinga	7,990.
JP-48	48"	Rosewood	7,990.
JP-52	52"	Polished Ebony	9,390.
JP-52	52"	Bubinga	9,990.
JP-52	52"	Rosewood	9,990.
Grands			
JP-175	5' 9"	Polished Ebony	17,390.
JP-175	5' 9"	Polished Ebony with Pommele Inlay	18,190.
JP-175	5' 9"	Polished Red Mahogany	18,990.
JP-175	5' 9"	Polished Brown Mahogany	18,990.
JP-175	5' 9"	Polished Kewazinga Bubinga	20,590.
JP-185	6' 1"	Polished Ebony	21,990.
JP-185	6' 1"	Polished Ebony with Pommele Inlay	22,990.
JP-185	6' 1"	Polished Red Mahogany	23,990.
JP-185	6' 1"	Polished Brown Mahogany	23,990.
JP-185	6' 1"	Polished Kewazinga Bubinga	25,990.
JP-185	6' 1"	Polished Santos Rosewood	27,990.
JP-185	6' 1"	Polished African Pommele	28,990.
JP-208	6' 10"	Polished Ebony	25,990.
JP-208	6' 10"	Polished Ebony with Pommele Inlay	27,190.
JP-208	6' 10"	Polished Kewazinga Bubinga	30,990.
JP-208	6' 10"	Polished Santos Rosewood	32,990.
JP-208	6' 10"	Polished African Pommele	34,500.

***For explanation of terms and prices, please see pages 20–25.**

QRS / Pianomation

Prices for Pianomation systems vary by piano manufacturer, installer, and accessories. The following are approximate retail prices from QRS. The usual dealer discounts may apply, especially as an incentive to purchase a piano.

Pianomation:	2000C Player System	4,000. to 5,000.
	2000CD+ Player System, incl. speaker	4,500. to 5,500.
	AMC Player System with CD and floppy drives, speaker (higher price would also include Record option and mute rail)	5,000. to 6,800.
Playola:	With 2000C Player System	3,600.
	With 2000CD+ Player System	4,000.
Practice Session:	Lite (LiteSwitch Record, Piano-Only sound, mute rail)	950.
	Opti (OptiScan Record, Piano-Only sound, mute rail)	1,400.
	Lite AMC (LiteSwitch Record, AMC, mute rail)	1,600.
	Opti AMC (OptiScan Record, AMC, mute rail)	1,950.

Ridgewood

Grands

152	5'	Polished Ebony	8,490.
152	5'	Polished Mahogany	8,890.
165	5' 5"	Polished Ebony	9,190.

Rieger-Kloss

Prices do not include bench.

Verticals

R-121	48"	Polished Ebony	5,490.
R-122	48"	Demi-Chippendale Polished Ebony	6,190.
R-122	48"	Demi-Chippendale Polished Walnut	6,190.
R-122	48"	Demi-Chippendale Polished Mahogany	6,190.

Model	Size	Style and Finish	Price*
R-122C	48"	Chippendale Polished Mahogany	6,690.
R-122C	48"	Chippendale Walnut and Pol. Walnut	6,690.
R-122R	48"	"Romance" Polished Ebony	6,870.
R-123	48"	Polished Ebony	6,090.
R-123	48"	Walnut	6,190.
R-123	48"	Polished Walnut	6,090.
R-123	48"	Polished Mahogany	6,090.
R-123	48"	Cherry	6,190.
R-125	50"	Polished Ebony	7,790.
R-125	50"	Polished Mahogany	7,990.
R-125	50"	Cherry	7,990.
R-126	50"	Polished Ebony	6,790.
R-126	50"	Polished Walnut	6,990.
R-126	50"	Cherry	6,990.
R-132	52"	Polished Ebony	8,790.
Grands			
RG-158	5' 2"	Polished Ebony	19,390.
RG-158	5' 2"	Polished Walnut	19,790.
RG-158	5' 2"	Polished Mahogany	19,790.
RG-158	5' 2"	*Polished White*	
RG-158C	5' 2"	Chippendale Polished Mahogany	23,190.
RG-158C	5' 2"	Chippendale Polished Walnut	23,190.
RG-185	6' 1"	Polished Ebony	22,490.
RG-185	6' 1"	Polished Walnut	23,190.
RG-185	6' 1"	Polished Mahogany	23,190.
RG-185	6' 1"	*Polished White*	
RG-210	6' 11"	Polished Ebony	29,990.
RG-272	8' 11"	Polished Ebony	53,990.

Ritmüller

Verticals

UP-110R2	43-1/2"	"Elegant" Continental Polished Ebony	3,090.
UP-110R2	43-1/2"	"Elegant" Continental Pol. Mahogany	3,140.
UP-110R2	43-1/2"	"Elegant" Continental Polished Walnut	3,140.
UP-110R2	43-1/2"	"Elegant" Continental Polished White	3,140.
UP-110R3	43-1/2"	"Designer" Continental Polished Ebony	3,090.

***For explanation of terms and prices, please see pages 20–25.**

Model	Size	Style and Finish	Price*

Ritmüller (continued)

Model	Size	Style and Finish	Price*
UP-110R3	43-1/2"	"Designer" Continental Mahogany	3,140.
UP-110R3	43-1/2"	"Designer" Continental Pol. Mahogany	3,140.
UP-110R3	43-1/2"	"Designer" Continental Pol. Walnut	3,140.
UP-118R1	46-1/2"	"Designer" Polished Ebony	3,620.
UP-118R1	46-1/2"	"Designer" Polished Mahogany	3,700.
UP-118R1	46-1/2"	"Designer" Polished Walnut	3,700.
UP-118R2	46-1/2"	"Scandinavian Design" Polished Ebony	3,620.
UP-118R2	46-1/2"	"Scandinavian Design" Pol. Catalpa	3,900.
UP-120R	48"	Polished Ebony	3,920.
UP-120R	48"	Polished Mahogany	3,980.
UP-120R	48"	Polished Walnut	3,980.
UP-120R	48"	Polished White	3,980.
UP-120R1	48"	"Designer European" Polished Ebony	4,040.
UP-120R1	48"	"Classic European" Pol. Blue-Green	4,090.
UP-120R2	48"	Chippendale Mahogany	4,390.
UP-120R2	48"	Chippendale Walnut	4,390.
UP-126R	49"	Polished Ebony w/ Medrone Burl Trim	5,170.
UP-130R	51"	Polished Ebony	5,400.
UP-130R	51"	Polished Mahogany	5,460.
UP-130R	51"	Walnut	5,460.
UP-130R	51"	Polished Ebony	4,700.
Grands			
GP-142R	4' 7"	"Kleine" Polished Ebony	8,630.
GP-142R	4' 7"	"Kleine" Polished Mahogany	8,980.
GP-142R	4' 7"	"Kleine" Polished Walnut	8,980.
GP-142R	4' 7"	"Kleine" Polished White	8,980.
GP-159R	5' 3"	Polished Ebony	11,560.
GP-159R	5' 3"	Polished Mahogany	11,880.
GP-159R	5' 3"	Polished Walnut	11,880.
GP-159R	5' 3"	Polished Cherry	11,880.
GP-159R	5' 3"	Polished White	11,880.
GP-159R1	5' 3"	Polished Ebony	11,360.
GP-159R1	5' 3"	Polished Mahogany	11,680.
GP-159R1	5' 3"	Polished Walnut	11,680.
GP-159R1	5' 3"	Polished White	11,680.

Model	Size	Style and Finish	Price*
GP-183R	6'	Polished Ebony	14,440.
GP-183R	6'	Polished Mahogany	14,760.
GP-183R	6'	Polished White	14,760.

Sagenhaft

Verticals

S-112	44-1/2"	Continental Polished Ebony	2,460.
S-112	44-1/2"	Continental Polished Mahogany	2,560.

Samick

Verticals

JS 042	42-1/2"	Continental Polished Ebony	2,590.
JS 042	42-1/2"	Continental Cherry	2,690.
JS 042	42-1/2"	Continental Walnut	2,690.
JS 042	42-1/2"	Continental Mahogany	2,690.
JS 042	42-1/2"	Continental Oak	2,690.
JS 042	42-1/2"	Continental Polished Ivory	2,590.
JS 042	42-1/2"	Continental Polished White	2,590.
JS 044T	44"	Cherry	3,390.
JS 044T	44"	Mahogany	3,390.
JS 044M	44"	Mediterranean Brown Oak	3,290.
JS 044F	44"	French Provincial Brown Oak	3,390.
JS 044F	44"	French Provincial Cherry	3,390.
JS 115	45"	Polished Ebony	2,790.
JS 115	45"	Cherry	2,890.
JS 115	45"	Walnut	2,890.
JS 115	45"	Mahogany	2,890.
JS 115	45"	Oak	2,890.
JS 115	45"	Polished Ivory	2,790.
JS 115	45"	Polished White	2,790.
JS 118T	46-1/2"	Cherry	3,990.
JS 118T	46-1/2"	Mahogany	3,990.
JS 118M	46-1/2"	Mediterranean Brown Oak	3,790.
JS 118F	46-1/2"	French Provincial Brown Oak	3,990.
JS 118F	46-1/2"	French Provincial Cherry	3,990.

***For explanation of terms and prices, please see pages 20–25.**

Model	Size	Style and Finish	Price*
Samick (continued)			
SU-147S	46-1/2"	Ebony and Polished Ebony	4,390.
SU-147S	46-1/2"	Walnut and Polished Walnut	4,590.
SU-147S	46-1/2"	Mahogany and Polished Mahogany	4,590.
SU-147S	46-1/2"	Oak and Polished Oak	4,590.
SU-118FA	46-1/2"	French Polished Mahogany	5,190.
SU-118FA	46-1/2"	French Polished Walnut	5,190.
WSU-118T	46-1/2"	"World" Polished Cherry	5,190.
WSU-118T	46-1/2"	"World" Polished Mahogany	5,190.
WSU-118F	46-1/2"	"World" French Polished Cherry	5,190.
JS 121F	48"	Polished Ebony	3,990.
JS 121F	48"	Polished Mahogany	4,190.
JS 121M	48"	Polished Ebony	3,890.
JS 121M	48"	Polished Mahogany	4,090.
JS 121M	48"	Polished White	4,090.
SU-121B	48"	Ebony and Polished Ebony	4,590.
SU-121B	48"	Walnut and Polished Walnut	4,790.
SU-121B	48"	Mahogany and Polished Mahogany	4,790.
WSU-121SD	48"	"World" Polished Ebony	5,390.
WSU-121SD	48"	"World" Polished Mahogany	5,590.
SU-131B	52"	Ebony and Polished Ebony	5,390.
SU-131B	52"	Walnut and Polished Walnut	5,590.
SU-131B	52"	Mahogany and Polished Mahogany	5,590.
WSU-131MD	52"	"World" Polished Ebony	5,990.
WSU-131MD	52"	"World" Polished Mahogany	6,390.
Grands			
SIG 50	4' 11-1/2"	Polished Ebony	7,790.
SIG 50	4' 11-1/2"	Polished Mahogany	8,190.
SG-150C	4' 11-1/2"	Ebony and Polished Ebony	9,560.
SG-150C	4' 11-1/2"	Walnut and Polished Walnut	10,060.
SG-150C	4' 11-1/2"	Mahogany and Polished Mahogany	10,060.
SG-150C	4' 11-1/2"	Oak and Polished Oak	10,060.
SG-150C	4' 11-1/2"	Cherry	10,060.
SG-150C	4' 11-1/2"	Polished Ivory	9,560.
SG-150C	4' 11-1/2"	Polished White	9,560.
SG-150KAF	4' 11-1/2"	French Provincial (all of above finishes)	11,190.

Model	Size	Style and Finish	Price*
SG-150KBF	4' 11-1/2"	French Provincial (all of above finishes)	12,050.
SG-161	5' 3-1/2"	Ebony and Polished Ebony	11,120.
SG-161	5' 3-1/2"	Walnut and Polished Walnut	11,640.
SG-161	5' 3-1/2"	Mahogany and Polished Mahogany	11,640.
SG-161	5' 3-1/2"	Oak and Polished Oak	11,640.
SG-161	5' 3-1/2"	Cherry	11,640.
SG-161	5' 3-1/2"	Polished Ivory	11,120.
SG-161	5' 3-1/2"	Polished White	11,120.
SG-161KBF	5' 3-1/2"	French Provincial (all of above finishes)	13,260.
SG-172	5' 7"	Ebony and Polished Ebony	11,990.
SG-172	5' 7"	Walnut and Polished Walnut	12,500.
SG-172	5' 7"	Mahogany and Polished Mahogany	12,500.
SG-172	5' 7"	Oak and Polished Oak	12,500.
SG-172	5' 7"	Cherry	12,500.
SG-172	5' 7"	Polished Ivory	11,990.
SG-172	5' 7"	Polished White	11,990.
SG-172L	5' 7"	Empire Ebony and Polished Ebony	13,060.
SG-172L	5' 7"	Empire Mahogany and Pol. Mahogany	13,580.
WFG-172	5' 7"	"World" Ebony and Polished Ebony	19,100.
WFG-172	5' 7"	*"World" All other finishes*	20,000.
SG-185	6' 1"	Ebony and Polished Ebony	12,840.
SG-185	6' 1"	*All other finishes*	13,360.
SG-185L	6' 1"	Empire Ebony and Polished Ebony	13,920.
SG-185L	6' 1"	Empire Mahogany and Pol. Mahogany	14,430.
WFG-185	6' 1"	"World" Ebony and Polished Ebony	21,000.
WFG-185	6' 1"	*"World" All other finishes*	22,000.
WFG-185L	6' 1"	"World" Empire Ebony and Pol. Ebony	21,900.
WFG-185L	6' 1"	"World" Empire Mahog and Pol.Mahog	22,900.
WFG-205	6' 8"	"World" Ebony and Polished Ebony	24,000.
WFG-205	6' 8"	*"World" All other finishes*	25,000.
WFG-215	7'	"World" Ebony and Polished Ebony	25,000.
WFG-215	7'	*"World" All other finishes*	26,000.
WFG-225	7' 4"	"World" Ebony and Polished Ebony	27,000.
WFG-225	7' 4"	*"World" All other finishes*	28,000.
WFG-275	9' 1"	"World" Ebony and Polished Ebony	67,990.
WFG-275	9' 1"	"World" Wood Finishes	71,990.

***For explanation of terms and prices, please see pages 20–25.**

Model	Size	Style and Finish	Price*

Sängler & Söhne / Wieler

Verticals			
UP-108	43"	Continental Polished Ebony	2,500.
UP-108	43"	Continental Polished Mahogany	2,500.
UP-108	43"	Continental Polished Walnut	2,500.
UP-108	43"	Continental Polished White	2,500.
UP-108M2	43"	Chippendale Polished Ebony	2,750.
UP-108M2	43"	Chippendale Polished Brown Mahogany	2,750.
UP-108M2	43"	Chippendale Polished Walnut	2,750.
UP-110P	44"	French Provincial Polished Mahogany	2,990.
UP-110P	44"	French Provincial Polished Walnut	2,990.
UP-110R	44"	Fruitwood	2,990.
UP-110R	44"	Mahogany	2,990.
UP-115M	45"	Polished Ebony	2,790.
UP-115M	45"	Polished Brown Mahogany	2,790.
BLR-120	47"	Continental Polished Ebony	1,990.
BLR-120	47"	Continental Polished Mahogany	1,990.
Grands			
GP-159	5' 3"	Polished Ebony	8,590.

Sauter

Verticals			
122	48"	"Schulpiano" Beech	13,500.
122	48"	"Domino" Polished Ebony	15,880.
122	48"	"Domino" Pear	15,880.
122	48"	"Resonance" Cherry/Yew	17,950.
122	48"	"Vista" Polished Ebony	17,170.
122	48"	"Vista" Maple	16,300.
122	48"	"Vista" Pear	17,880.
122	48"	"Vista" Cherry	17,400.
122	48"	"M-Line M2" Polished Ebony	20,900.
128	50"	"M-Line M1" Polished Ebony	24,450.
130	51"	"Competence" Polished Ebony	19,800.

Model	Size	Style and Finish	Price*
Grands			
160	5' 3"	"Alpha" Polished Ebony	41,900.
160	5' 3"	"Alpha" Walnut	38,000.
160	5' 3"	"Alpha" Mahogany	38,000.
160	5' 3"	"Alpha" Polished White	43,250.
160	5' 3"	Chippendale Walnut	41,400.
160	5' 3"	Chippendale Mahogany	41,400.
160	5' 3"	Chippendale Cherry	44,700.
160	5' 3"	"Noblesse" Walnut	42,800.
160	5' 3"	"Noblesse" Mahogany	42,800.
160	5' 3"	"Noblesse" Cherry	46,100.
185	6' 1"	"Delta" Polished Ebony	45,750.
185	6' 1"	"Delta" Walnut	41,920.
185	6' 1"	"Delta" Mahogany	41,920.
185	6' 1"	Chippendale Walnut	46,720.
185	6' 1"	Chippendale Mahogany	46,720.
185	6' 1"	Chippendale Cherry	50,020.
185	6' 1"	"Noblesse" Walnut	48,920.
185	6' 1"	"Noblesse" Mahogany	48,920.
185	6' 1"	"Noblesse" Cherry	50,520.
220	7' 2"	"Omega" Polished Ebony	58,500.
220	7' 2"	"Omega" Walnut	54,900.
220	7' 2"	"Omega" Mahogany	54,900.
275	9'	"Concert" Polished Ebony	99,590.
Satin models		*Additional, for polished finish*	5,400.
Peter Maly models		*Available by special order only*	on request

Schimmel

Verticals			
112 S	45"	*"School" Open-Pore Ebony*	12,580.
112 S	45"	"School" Open-Pore Walnut	12,580.
112 S	45"	"School" Open-Pore Oak	12,580.
116 E	46"	"Exquisite" Polished Ebony	12,780.
116 E	46"	"Exquisite" Polished Mahogany	13,180.
116 E	46"	*"Exquisite" Polished White*	13,180.
116 E	46"	"Exquisite" Alder	13,180.

***For explanation of terms and prices, please see pages 20–25.**

Model	Size	Style and Finish	Price*

Schimmel (continued)

116 E	46"	"Exquisite" Open-Pore Walnut	13,180.
116 E	46"	"Exquisite" Open-Pore Beech	13,180.
116 E	46"	"Exquisite" Open-Pore Maple	13,180.
116 E	46"	"Exquisite" Open-Pore Ash	13,180.
116 E	46"	"Exquisite" Waxed Plum	13,180.
116 E	46"	"Exquisite" O.P. Waxed Swiss Pear	13,180.
116 S	46"	"Special" Polished Ebony	11,380.
116 S	46"	"Special" Alder	11,980.
116 S	46"	"Special" Open-Pore Walnut	11,980.
116 S	46"	"Special" Open-Pore Birch	11,980.
116 S	46"	"Special" Open-Pore Beech	11,980.
116 S	46"	"Special" Waxed Swiss Pear	11,980.
120 I	48"	"International" Polished Ebony	12,880.
120 M	48"	"Solid" Open-Pore Waxed Maple	14,280.
120 RI	48"	"Royale Intarsia" Polished Mahogany	15,580.
120 RI	48"	*"Royale Intarsia" Polished Cherry*	15,980.
120 S	48"	*"School" Open-Pore Ebony*	12,980.
120 S	48"	"School" Open-Pore Oak	12,980.
120 TN	48"	"Noblesse" Polished Ebony	13,380.
120 TN	48"	*"Noblesse" Polished White*	13,980.
120 TN-SE	48"	"Noblesse" Sig. Ed. Polished Ebony	13,580.
120 TR	48"	"Residence" Polished Ebony	13,580.
120 TR	48"	"Residence" O.P. Waxed Swiss Pear	13,980.
122 KE	49"	"Classicism Exquisite" Polished Ebony	13,380.
122 KE	49"	"Classicism Exquisite" Pol. Mahogany	13,780.
122 KE	49"	*"Classicism Exquisite" Polished Cherry*	14,180.
122 KE	49"	*"Classicism Exquisite" O.P. Wax Alder*	13,780.
F 122 AC	49"	"Art Cubus" Polished Ebony	15,500.
F 122 AC	49"	"Art Cubus" Waxed Swiss Pear	15,900.
F 122 SE	49"	"Salon Exquisite" Polished Ebony	14,700.
S 125 DN	49"	"Diamond Noblesse" Polished Ebony	17,180.
S 125 DN	49"	"Diamond Noblesse" Polished Mahog.	17,580.
S 125 DP	49"	"Diamond Prestige" Polished Ebony	17,580.
S 125 DP	49"	"Diamond Prestige" Pol. Mahogany	17,980.
130 T	51"	Polished Ebony	15,380.

Model	Size	Style and Finish	Price*
130 T	51"	Polished Mahogany	15,780.
130 T	51"	*Polished Walnut*	15,780.
130 T	51"	*Polished White*	15,780.
130 T-O	51"	Polished Ebony (upper panel oval inlay)	15,980.
O 132 DT	52"	Polished Ebony	18,200.
O 132 DT	52"	Polished Mahogany	18,800.

Grands

When not mentioned, satin finish available on special order at same price as high-polish finish.

SP 182 C	6'	*Chippendale Polished Walnut*	38,380.
SP 182 C	6'	*Chippendale Polished Mahogany*	38,380.
SP 182 DE	6'	"Diamond" Polished Ebony	38,980.
SP 182 DE	6'	"Diamond" Polished White	42,980.
SP 182 DE	6'	"Diamond" Polished Pyramid Mahog.	42,980.
SP 182 DE	6'	"Diamond" Polished Bubinga	42,980.
SP 182 DE	6'	*"Diamond" Polished Bird's Eye Maple*	42,980.
SP 182 DE	6'	*"Diamond" Polished Swiss Pear*	42,980.
SP 182 DE	6'	"Diamond" Macassar	42,980.
SP 182 E	6'	Empire Polished Pyramid Mahogany	42,980.
SP 182 S	6'	*"School" Open-Pore Oak*	33,780.
SP 182 T	6'	Polished Ebony	34,580.
SP 182 T	6'	*Polished Walnut*	35,380.
SP 182 T	6'	Polished Mahogany	35,380.
SP 182 T	6'	*Polished White*	35,380.
SP 182 TE	6'	"Exquisite" Polished Ebony	36,180.
SP 182 TE	6'	"Exquisite" Polished Mahogany	36,980.
SP 182 TE	6'	"Exquisite" Polished White	36,980.
SP 182 TE-I	6'	"Exquisite" Polished Mahogany Intarsia	38,180.
SP 182 TJ	6'	"Jubilee" Polished Ebony	36,580.
SP 182 TJ	6'	"Jubilee" Polished Mahogany	37,580.
SP 182 TJ	6'	*"Jubilee" Polished White*	37,580.
SP 182 TJ	6'	*"Jubilee" Polished Swiss Pear*	37,580.
208 P	6' 10"	*"Pegasus"*	169,800.
CC 213 A	7'	*Art Edition*	117,800.
CC 213 DE	7'	"Diamond" Polished Ebony	43,980.
CC 213 DE	7'	"Diamond" Polished White	47,980.
CC 213 DE	7'	"Diamond" Polished Pyramid Mahog.	47,980.

***For explanation of terms and prices, please see pages 20–25.**

Model	Size	Style and Finish	Price*

Schimmel (continued)

CC 213 DE	7'	"Diamond" Polished Bubinga	47,980.
CC 213 DE	7'	*"Diamond" Polished Bird's Eye Maple*	47,980.
CC 213 DE	7'	*"Diamond" Polished Swiss Pear*	47,980.
CC 213 DE	7'	"Diamond" Macassar	47,980.
CC 213 G	7'	*Plexiglas*	97,800.
CC 213 S	7'	*"School" Open-Pore Oak*	38,980.
CC 213 T	7'	Polished Ebony	40,180.
CC 213 T	7'	Polished Mahogany	40,980.
CC 213 T	7'	*Polished White*	40,980.
CC 213 T	7'	*Polished Walnut*	40,980.
CC 213 TE	7'	"Exquisite" Polished Ebony	41,780.
CC 213 TE	7'	"Exquisite" Polished Mahogany	42,780.
CC 213 TE	7'	"Exquisite" Polished White	42,780.
CC 213 TJ	7'	*"Jubilee" Polished Ebony*	42,180.
CC 213 TJ	7'	*"Jubilee" Polished Mahogany*	43,180.
CC 213 TJ	7'	*"Jubilee" Polished White*	43,180.
CC 213 TJ	7'	*"Jubilee" Polished Swiss Pear*	43,180.
CO 256 T	8' 4"	Polished Ebony	59,800.

Schubert

Verticals

B-21	43"	Continental Polished Ebony	2,260.
B-21	43"	Continental Polished Cherry	2,230.
B-21	43"	Continental Polished Walnut	2,230
B-21	43"	Continental Polished Oak	2,230.
B-20	44"	Country French Oak	2,390.
B-20	44"	French Provincial Mahogany	2,390.
B-22	44"	Polished Ebony	2,320.
B-22	44"	Polished Mahogany	2,290.
B-22	44"	Oak	2,320.
B-22	44"	Polished Oak	2,290.
B-23	44"	Chippendale Polished Ebony	2,440.
B-23	44"	Chippendale Polished Walnut	2,440.
B-23	44"	Chippendale Oak	2,440.

Model	Size	Style and Finish	Price*
B-23	44"	Chippendale Polished Oak	2,440.
B-23	44"	Chippendale Polished Cherry	2,440.
B-15	47"	Polished Ebony	2,398.
B-15	47"	Polished Mahogany	2,350.
B-15	47"	Polished Walnut	2,350.
B-15	47"	Polished Oak	2,350.
A-120-2	47"	Chippendale Polished Ebony	2,690.
A-120-2	47"	Chippendale Polished Walnut	2,690.
A-120-2	47"	Chippendale Polished Oak	2,690.
A-120-2	47"	Chippendale Polished Cherry	2,690.

Schultz & Sons

Model numbers beginning with 3 or 4 designate pianos manufactured by Broadwood, numbers beginning with 7 or 8, by Samick.

Verticals

3807-S	47"	Polished Ebony	19,195.
3807-S	47"	Walnut	18,150.
3807-S	47"	Polished Walnut	20,395.
3807-S	47"	Mahogany	18,150.
3807-S	47"	Polished Mahogany	20,395.
3809-S	47"	Mahogany	24,150.
3809-S	47"	Polished Mahogany	25,150.
3819-S	47"	Walnut	20,550.
3819-S	47"	Polished Walnut	22,595.
3819-S	47"	Mahogany	20,550.
3819-S	47"	Polished Mahogany	22,595.
7708-S	47-1/2"	Polished Mahogany	10,550.
7708-S	47-1/2"	Polished Cherry	10,550.
7708-SCC	47-1/2"	*Custom Finish*	13,550.
7703-S	47-1/2"	Polished Mahogany	10,550.
7703-S	47-1/2"	Polished Cherry	10,550.
7703-SCC	47-1/2"	*Custom Finish*	13,550.
7707-U	48-1/2"	Ebony and Polished Ebony	11,250.
7707-U	48-1/2"	Walnut and Polished Walnut	12,095.
7707-U	48-1/2"	Polished Mahogany	12,095.

***For explanation of terms and prices, please see pages 20–25.**

Model	Size	Style and Finish	Price*

Schultz & Sons (continued)

3817-U	50"	Polished Ebony	25,150.
3817-U	50"	Walnut	23,595.
3817-U	50"	Polished Walnut	26,395.
3817-U	50"	Mahogany	23,595.
3817-U	50"	Polished Mahogany	26,395.
7717-U	52"	Ebony and Polished Ebony	12,095.
7717-U	52"	Walnut and Polished Walnut	12,850.
7717-U	52"	Polished Mahogany	12,850.
Grands			
8501-B	5' 2"	Ebony and Polished Ebony	18,050.
8501-B	5' 2"	Walnut and Polished Walnut	19,050.
8501-B	5' 2"	Polished Mahogany	19,050.
8501-B	5' 2"	Polished Ivory	18,450.
8501-B	5' 2"	Polished White	18,450.
8601-B	5' 2"	Ebony and Polished Ebony	25,695.
8601-B	5' 2"	Walnut and Polished Walnut	26,550.
8601-B	5' 2"	Polished Mahogany	26,550.
8601-B	5' 2"	Polished Ivory	25,795.
8601-B	5' 2"	Polished White	25,795.
8601-M	5' 9-1/2"	"Classic" Ebony and Polished Ebony	20,295.
8601-M	5' 9-1/2"	"Classic" Walnut and Polished Walnut	21,250.
8601-M	5' 9-1/2"	"Classic" Polished Mahogany	21,250.
8601-M	5' 9-1/2"	"Classic" Polished Ivory	20,795.
8601-M	5' 9-1/2"	"Classic" Polished White	20,795.
8701-M	5' 9-1/2"	"Classic" Ebony and Polished Ebony	26,995.
8701-M	5' 9-1/2"	"Classic" Walnut and Polished Walnut	27,950.
8701-M	5' 9-1/2"	"Classic" Polished Mahogany	27,950.
8701-M	5' 9-1/2"	"Classic" Polished Ivory	27,495.
8701-M	5' 9-1/2"	"Classic" Polished White	27,495.
8721-M	5' 9-1/2"	"Victorian" Ebony and Polished Ebony	22,450.
8721-M	5' 9-1/2"	"Victorian" Walnut and Pol. Walnut	23,550.
8721-M	5' 9-1/2"	"Victorian" Polished Mahogany	23,550.
8721-M	5' 9-1/2"	"Victorian" Polished Ivory	23,050.
8721-M	5' 9-1/2"	"Victorian" Polished White	23,050.
8821-M	5' 9-1/2"	"Victorian" Ebony and Polished Ebony	29,395.

Model	Size	Style and Finish	Price*
8821-M	5' 9-1/2"	"Victorian" Walnut and Pol. Walnut	30,295.
8821-M	5' 9-1/2"	"Victorian" Polished Mahogany	30,295.
8821-M	5' 9-1/2"	"Victorian" Polished Ivory	29,550.
8821-M	5' 9-1/2"	"Victorian" Polished White	29,550.
8741-M	5' 9-1/2"	Polished Mahogany with Floral Inlays	28,495.
8741-MCC	5' 9-1/2"	*Custom Finish with Floral Inlays*	35,250.
8741-MCS	5' 9-1/2"	*Custom Finish with Custom Inlays*	on request
8731-M	5' 9-1/2"	Louis XV Ebony and Polished Ebony	25,595.
8731-M	5' 9-1/2"	Louis XV Walnut and Polished Walnut	26,550.
8731-M	5' 9-1/2"	Louis XV Polished Mahogany	26,550.
8731-M	5' 9-1/2"	Louis XV Polished Ivory	26,050.
8731-M	5' 9-1/2"	Louis XV Polished White	26,050.
4908-L	6'	"Euro Classic" Ebony	67,795.
4908-L	6'	"Euro Classic" Polished Ebony	64,995.
8701-L	6' 1"	"Classic" Ebony and Polished Ebony	21,695.
8701-L	6' 1"	"Classic" Walnut and Polished Walnut	22,595.
8701-L	6' 1"	"Classic" Polished Mahogany	22,595.
8701-L	6' 1"	"Classic" Polished Ivory	21,995.
8701-L	6' 1"	"Classic" Polished White	21,995.
8801-L	6' 1"	"Classic" Ebony and Polished Ebony	28,550.
8801-L	6' 1"	"Classic" Walnut and Polished Walnut	29,450.
8801-L	6' 1"	"Classic" Polished Mahogany	29,450.
8801-L	6' 1"	"Classic" Polished Ivory	28,795.
8801-L	6' 1"	"Classic" Polished White	28,795.
8709-L	6' 1"	"Victorian" Ebony and Polished Ebony	23,895.
8709-L	6' 1"	"Victorian" Walnut and Pol. Walnut	25,050.
8709-L	6' 1"	"Victorian" Polished Mahogany	25,050.
8709-L	6' 1"	"Victorian" Polished Ivory	24,395.
8709-L	6' 1"	"Victorian" Polished White	24,395.
8809-L	6' 1"	"Victorian" Ebony and Polished Ebony	31,495.
8809-L	6' 1"	"Victorian" Walnut and Pol. Walnut	32,550.
8809-L	6' 1"	"Victorian" Polished Mahogany	32,550.
8809-L	6' 1"	"Victorian" Polished Ivory	32,695.
8809-L	6' 1"	"Victorian" Polished White	32,695.
8811-X	6' 9"	Ebony and Polished Ebony	38,595.
8811-SX	7' 1"	Ebony and Polished Ebony	43,395.

***For explanation of terms and prices, please see pages 20–25.**

Model	Size	Style and Finish	Price*

Schulze Pollmann

Verticals			
113E	45"	Polished Ebony	6,590.
113E	45"	Polished Briar Mahogany	7,190.
113E	45"	Polished Peacock Mahogany	7,190.
113E	45"	Polished Briar Walnut	7,190.
113E	45"	Polished Peacock Walnut	7,190.
113E	45"	Polished White	6,590.
118	46"	Polished Ebony	7,990.
118	46"	Polished Briar Walnut	8,990.
118	46"	Polished Briar Mahogany	8,990.
126P6	50"	Polished Ebony	9,990.
126P6	50"	Polished Ebony with Gold Borders	10,380.
126P6	50"	Polished Peacock Natural Cherry	10,790.
126P6	50"	Oval Feather Mahogany	10,790.
126P6	50"	Polished Mahogany	10,790.
126P6	50"	Polished Briar Mahogany	10,790.
126P6	50"	Polished Peacock Mahogany	10,790.
126P6	50"	Walnut and Polished Walnut	10,790.
126P6	50"	Satin and Polished Peacock Walnut	10,790.
126P6	50"	Briar Walnut and Polished Briar Walnut	10,790.
Grands			
160A	5' 3"	Polished Ebony	20,790.
160A	5' 3"	Polished Mahogany	21,990.
160A	5' 3"	Polished Walnut	21,990.
160GK	5' 3"	Chippendale Polished Ebony	25,990.
160GK	5' 3"	Chippendale Polished Mahogany	25,990.
190F	6' 3"	Polished Ebony	29,760.
190F	6' 2"	Polished Briar Mahogany	33,760.
190F	6' 2"	Polished Walnut	31,990.
197A	6' 7"	Polished Ebony	35,780.
197A	6' 7"	Polished Mahogany	39,780.
197A	6' 7"	Polished Walnut	39,780.

Model	Size	Style and Finish	Price*

Seidl & Sohn

Prices do not include bench.

Verticals

SL 109	43"	Continental Polished Ebony	5,014.
SL 109	43"	Continental Open-Pore Walnut	4,784.
SL 109	43"	Continental Polished Walnut	5,014.
SL 109	43"	Continental Polished Flame Mahogany	5,014.
SL 109	43"	Continental Polished White	5,175.
SL 113	46"	Polished Ebony	5,198.
SL 113	46"	Open-Pore Walnut	4,945.
SL 113	46"	Polished Walnut	5,198.
SL 113	46"	Polished Flame Mahogany	5,198.
SL 113	46"	Polished White	5,359.
SL 117	47"	Chippendale Polished Walnut	5,819.
SL 120	48"	Polished Ebony	5,589.
SL 120	48"	Open-Pore Walnut	5,313.
SL 120	48"	Polished Walnut	5,589.
SL 120	48"	Polished Flame Mahogany	5,589.
SL 120	48"	Polished White	5,773.
SL 127	51"	Polished Ebony	6,716.

Seiler

Verticals

116	46"	"Mondial" Open-Pore Ebony	13,500.
116	46"	"Mondial" Open-Pore Walnut	13,500.
116	46"	"Mondial" Open-Pore Mahogany	13,500.
116	46"	"Mondial" Polished Mahogany	14,120.
116	46"	"Mondial" Open-Pore Oak	13,500.
116	46"	"Mondial" Open-Pore Cherry	14,120.
116	46"	"Jubilee" Polished Ebony	14,480.
116	46"	"Jubilee" Polished White	14,720.
116	46"	Chippendale Open-Pore Walnut	13,620.
116	46"	"Escorial" Open-Pore Cherry, Intarsia	14,720.
122	48"	"Konsole" Open-Pore Ebony	14,040.
122	48"	"Konsole" Polished Ebony	15,000.

***For explanation of terms and prices, please see pages 20–25.**

Model	Size	Style and Finish	Price*

Seiler (continued)

122	48"	"Konsole" Open-Pore Walnut	14,040.
122	48"	"Konsole" Polished Walnut Rootwood	17,340.
122	48"	"Konsole" Open-Pore Oak	14,040.
122	48"	"Konsole" Open-Pore Cherry	14,740.
122	48"	"Konsole" Polished Brown Ash	17,340.
122	48"	"Konsole" Maple Burl	14,600.
122	48"	"Konsole" Polished White	15,380.
122	48"	"School" Open-Pore Ebony	13,400.
122	48"	"School" Open-Pore Walnut	13,400.
122	48"	"School" Open-Pore Oak	13,400.
122	48"	"Vienna" Polished Ebony w/Pilaster	15,400.
122	48"	"Vienna" Pol. Ebony w/Pilaster & Oval	15,560.
122	48"	"Vienna" Pol. Mahog. w/ Flower Inlays	17,340.
122	48"	"Vienna" Pol. Walnut w/ Flower Inlays	17,340.
132	52"	"Concert SMR" Polished Ebony	19,180.
132	52"	"Concert SMR" Pol. Ebony w/Oval	19,760.
132	52"	"Concert SMR" Pol. Ebony w/Candle	19,740.
132	52"	"Concert SMR" Pol. Ebony w/Panels	19,880.
132	52"	"Concert SMR" Open-Pore Walnut	18,620.
132	52"	"Concert SMR" Polished Mahogany	19,780.
132	52"	"Limited Edition" Polished Ebony	22,120.
132	52"	"Lim. Edit." Pol. Eb. w/Oval or Pilaster	22,580.
132	52"	"Lim. Edit." Pol. Eb. w/Oval & Pilaster	23,040.
Grands			
180	5' 11"	"Maestro" Polished Ebony	39,400.
180	5' 11"	"Maestro" Open-Pore Walnut	39,400.
180	5' 11"	"Maestro" Polished Walnut	42,040.
180	5' 11"	"Maestro" Open-Pore Mahogany	39,400.
180	5' 11"	"Maestro" Polished Mahogany	42,040.
180	5' 11"	"Maestro" Polished Pyramid Mahogany	55,200.
180	5' 11"	"Maestro" Polished Burl Rosewood	49,200.
180	5' 11"	"Maestro" Polished White	40,280.
180	5' 11"	Chippendale Open-Pore Walnut	41,940.
180	5' 11"	"Westminster" Pol. Mahogany, Intarsia	55,200.
180	5' 11"	"Florenz" Pol. Walnut/Myrtle, Intarsia	55,200.

Model	Size	Style and Finish	Price*
180	5' 11"	"Florenz" Pol. Mahog./Myrtle, Intarsia	55,200.
180	5' 11"	"Louvre" Polished Ebony	44,240.
180	5' 11"	"Louvre" Polished Cherry, Intarsia	55,200.
180	5' 11"	"Louvre" Polished White	45,000.
180	5' 11"	"Prado" Polished Brown Ash	56,760.
180	5' 11"	"Prado" Polished Burl Redwood	56,760.
180	5' 11"	"Stella" Pol. Maple Rootwood, Intarsia	67,800.
180	5' 11"	"Meridian" Pol. Maple Rootwd. Intarsia	67,800.
180	5' 11"	"Showmaster" Chrome/Brass/Polyester	109,960.
208	6' 9"	"Professional" Polished Ebony	44,360.
208	6' 9"	"Empire 1897" Open-Pore Blue w/Brass	153,040.
208	6' 9"	"Solitaire" Custom with Painting	172,480.
208	6' 9"	"Solitaire" Custom without Painting	140,040.
240	8'	"Concert" Polished Ebony	61,020.

Steinberg, Wilh.

Prices do not include bench.

Verticals

IQ 16	46"	Polished Ebony	8,050.
IQ 16	46"	"Amadeus" Polished Ebony	8,450.
IQ 16	46"	Beech	8,300.
IQ 16	46"	Oak	8,300.
IQ 16	46"	Alder	8,300.
IQ 16	46"	Walnut	8,300.
IQ 16	46"	Cherry	8,380.
IQ 16	46"	Mahogany	8,380.
IQ 16	46"	Cherry, Walnut, Mahogany with Inlay	8,580.
IQ 16	46"	Yew	8,900.
C 2	47"	Polished Ebony	7,900.
IQ 22	49"	Polished Ebony	8,800.
IQ 22	49"	"Amadeus" Polished Ebony	9,950.
IQ 22	49"	Beech	8,800.
IQ 22	49"	Oak	8,800.
IQ 22	49"	Alder	8,800.
IQ 22	49"	Walnut	8,800.
IQ 22	49"	Cherry	8,980.

***For explanation of terms and prices, please see pages 20–25.**

Model	Size	Style and Finish	Price*

Steinberg, Wilh. (continued)

IQ 22	49"	Mahogany	8,980.
IQ 22	49"	Cherry, Walnut, Mahogany with Inlay	9,500.
IQ 22	49"	Maple/Chromium	9,500.
IQ 22	49"	Yew	9,580.
IQ 28	52"	Polished Ebony	11,350.
IQ 28	52"	"Amadeus" Polished Ebony	11,900.
IQ 28	52"	Cherry, Walnut, Mahogany with Inlay	11,500.
IQ 28	52"	"Passione" Polished Ebony	12,950.
All models		Polyester Finish, add'l	700.
Grands			
IQ 77	5' 9"	Polished Ebony	28,600.
IQ 77	5' 9"	Cherry	28,600.
IQ 77	5' 9"	Mahogany	28,600.
IQ 77	5' 9"	Polyester Finish, add'l	700.

Steingraeber & Söhne

This list includes only those models most likely to be offered to U.S. customers. Other models, styles, and finishes are available.

Verticals			
122T	48"	French Cherry with Ebony Accents	21,800.
130	51"	Polished Ebony with "Twist" Panels	29,780.
138	54"	Polished Ebony	31,780.
Grands			
168N	5' 6"	Polished Ebony	47,700.
168K	5' 6"	"Classicism" Polished Ebony	56,530.
168K	5' 6"	"Classicism" Pol. Ebony w/Mahogany	63,500.
168K	5' 6"	"Classicism" Pol. Ebony w/Burl Walnut	63,500.
205N	6' 9"	Polished Ebony	64,490.
205K	6' 9"	"Classicism" Polished Ebony	72,880.

Model	Size	Style and Finish	Price*

Steinway & Sons

Model	Size	Style and Finish	Price*
Verticals			
4510	45"	Sheraton Ebony	17,800.
4510	45"	Sheraton Mahogany	19,600.
4510	45"	Sheraton Walnut	20,300.
4510	45"	Sheraton Dark Cherry	20,900.
1098	46-1/2"	Ebony	16,900.
1098	46-1/2"	Mahogany	18,100.
1098	46-1/2"	Walnut	18,800.
K-52	52"	Ebony	22,100.
K-52	52"	Mahogany	24,900.
K-52	52"	Walnut	25,600.
Grands			
S	5' 1"	Ebony	36,300.
S	5' 1"	Mahogany	40,600.
S	5' 1"	Walnut	41,800.
S	5' 1"	Figured Sapele	44,100.
S	5' 1"	Kewazinga Bubinga	45,300.
S	5' 1"	East Indian Rosewood	51,400.
S	5' 1"	Santos Rosewood	50,500.
S	5' 1"	African Pommele	51,800.
S	5' 1"	Macassar Ebony	56,700.
S	5' 1"	Dark Cherry	44,400.
S	5' 1"	Hepplewhite Dark Cherry	45,500.
M	5' 7"	Ebony	39,400.
M	5' 7"	Mahogany	44,100.
M	5' 7"	Walnut	45,300.
M	5' 7"	Figured Sapele	47,200.
M	5' 7"	Kewazinga Bubinga	49,500.
M	5' 7"	East Indian Rosewood	55,400.
M	5' 7"	Santos Rosewood	54,400.
M	5' 7"	African Pommele	55,700.
M	5' 7"	Macassar Ebony	61,000.
M	5' 7"	Dark Cherry	47,600.
M	5' 7"	Hepplewhite Dark Cherry	49,700.

***For explanation of terms and prices, please see pages 20–25.**

Model	Size	Style and Finish	Price*

Steinway & Sons (continued)

M SK-1014A	5' 7"	Chippendale Mahogany	53,800.
M SK-1014A	5' 7"	Chippendale Walnut	55,200.
M SK-501A	5' 7"	Louis XV Walnut	70,400.
M SK-501A	5' 7"	Louis XV East Indian Rosewood	81,700.
L	5' 10-1/2"	Ebony	43,900.
L	5' 10-1/2"	Mahogany	49,500.
L	5' 10-1/2"	Walnut	50,500.
L	5' 10-1/2"	Figured Sapele	52,700.
L	5' 10-1/2"	Kewazinga Bubinga	55,400.
L	5' 10-1/2"	East Indian Rosewood	62,600.
L	5' 10-1/2"	Santos Rosewood	61,600.
L	5' 10-1/2"	African Pommele	62,900.
L	5' 10-1/2"	Macassar Ebony	68,400.
L	5' 10-1/2"	Dark Cherry	53,200.
L	5' 10-1/2"	Hepplewhite Dark Cherry	55,800.
A	6' 2"	Limited Edition Tricentennial Pol. Eby.	75,700.
B	6' 10-1/2"	Ebony	55,200.
B	6' 10-1/2"	Mahogany	62,600.
B	6' 10-1/2"	Walnut	63,900.
B	6' 10-1/2"	Figured Sapele	66,900.
B	6' 10-1/2"	Kewazinga Bubinga	70,000.
B	6' 10-1/2"	East Indian Rosewood	78,900.
B	6' 10-1/2"	Santos Rosewood	77,800.
B	6' 10-1/2"	African Pommele	79,300.
B	6' 10-1/2"	Macassar Ebony	86,200.
B	6' 10-1/2"	Dark Cherry	68,200.
B	6' 10-1/2"	Hepplewhite Dark Cherry	70,800.
D	8' 11-3/4"	Ebony	83,120.
D	8' 11-3/4"	Mahogany	91,000.
D	8' 11-3/4"	Walnut	92,400.
D	8' 11-3/4"	Figured Sapele	96,600.
D	8' 11-3/4"	Kewazinga Bubinga	100,600.
D	8' 11-3/4"	East Indian Rosewood	112,800.
D	8' 11-3/4"	Santos Rosewood	111,800.
D	8' 11-3/4"	African Pommele	113,100.

Model	Size	Style and Finish	Price*
D	8' 11-3/4"	Macassar Ebony	123,500.
D	8' 11-3/4"	Dark Cherry	98,400.
D	8' 11-3/4"	Hepplewhite Dark Cherry	102,300.

Grands (Hamburg)

I frequently get requests for prices of pianos made in Steinway's branch factory in Hamburg, Germany. Officially, these pianos are not sold in North America, but it is possible to order one through an American Steinway dealer, or to go to Europe and purchase one there. The following list shows approximately how much it would cost to purchase a Hamburg Steinway in Germany and have it shipped to the United States. The list was derived by taking the published retail price in Germany, subtracting the value-added tax not applicable to foreign purchasers, converting to U.S. dollars (the rate used here is US$1.00 = DM2.30, but is obviously subject to change), and adding approximate charges for duty, air freight, crating, insurance, brokerage fees, and delivery. Only prices for grands in polished ebony are shown here. *Caution:* This list is published for general informational purposes only. The price that Steinway would charge for a piano ordered through an American Steinway dealer may be different. (Also, the cost of a trip to Germany to purchase the piano is not included!)

S-155	5' 1"	Polished Ebony	33,500.
M-170	5' 7"	Polished Ebony	36,800.
O-180	5' 10-1/2"	Polished Ebony	39,100.
A-188	6' 2"	Polished Ebony	41,700.
B-211	6' 11"	Polished Ebony	48,600.
C-227	7' 5-1/2"	Polished Ebony	56,900.
D-274	8' 11-3/4"	Polished Ebony *(estimated)*	72,700.

Story & Clark

Verticals

American	42"	Oak	4,700.
American	42"	Cherry	4,700.
Heirloom	42"	Queen Anne Oak	4,700.
Heirloom	42"	Queen Anne Cherry	4,700.
Southwest	42"	French Provincial White	4,700.
Century	42"	Italian Provincial Walnut	4,700.
Mediterranean	42"	Mediterranean Oak	4,700.

***For explanation of terms and prices, please see pages 20–25.**

Model	Size	Style and Finish	Price*

Story & Clark (continued)

Chippendale	42"	Chippendale Oak	4,900.
Chippendale	42"	Chippendale Cherry	4,900.
Prelude	44"	Continental Polished Ebony	2,790.
Prelude	44"	Continental Polished Mahogany	2,790.
Church	46"	Oak	4,990.
School	46"	Oak	4,990.
Grands			
Cambridge	4' 10"	Polished Ebony	8,790.
Prelude	5'	Polished Ebony	7,590.
Cambridge	5' 2"	Polished Ebony	9,790.
Cambridge	5' 2"	Polished Mahogany	9,790.
Prelude	5' 4"	Polished Ebony	9,800.
Hampton	5' 5"	Ebony	23,600.
Hampton	5' 5"	Cherry	23,600.
Hampton	5' 5"	with Inlays	28,000.
Cambridge	5' 6"	Polished Ebony	10,790.
Cambridge	5' 6"	Mahogany Inlay	11,590.
Cambridge	5' 6"	Polished Mahogany Inlay	11,590.

Strauss

Verticals			
UP-108E	42-1/2"	Polished Ebony	2,518.
UP-108E	42-1/2"	Polished Mahogany	2,518.
UP-108E	42-1/2"	Polished Walnut	2,518.
UP-110A	43-1/2"	Polished Ebony	2,598.
UP-110A	43-1/2"	Polished Mahogany	2,598.
UP-110A	43-1/2"	Polished Walnut	2,598.
UP-110GD	43-1/2"	Satin	2,998.
UP-110GE	43-1/2"	Satin	2,998.
UP-117D,C	46"	Polished Ebony	2,738.
UP-117D,C	46"	Polished Mahogany	2,738.
UP-117D,C	46"	Polished Walnut	2,738.
UP-118	46-1/2"	Polished Ebony	2,918.
UP-118	46-1/2"	Polished Mahogany	2,918.

Model	Size	Style and Finish	Price*
UP-118	46-1/2"	Polished Walnut	2,918.
UP-120E	47"	Satin	3,500.
UP-120H	47"	Polished Ebony	3,500.
UP-120E-2,3	47"	Polished Maple	3,750.
UP-122B	48"	Polished Ebony	3,198.
UP-122B	48"	Polished Mahogany	3,198.
UP-122B	48"	Polished Walnut	3,198.
Grands			
GP-170	5' 7"	Polished Ebony	9,198.

Walter, Charles R.

Verticals			
1520	43"	Oak	7,560.
1520	43"	Cherry	7,800.
1520	43"	Walnut	7,820.
1520	43"	Mahogany	7,960.
1520	43"	Riviera Oak	7,540.
1520	43"	Italian Provincial Oak	7,540.
1520	43"	Italian Provincial Walnut	7,840.
1520	43"	French Provincial Oak	7,840.
1520	43"	French Provincial Walnut	8,080.
1520	43"	French Provincial Cherry	8,100.
1520	43"	Country Classic Oak	7,600.
1520	43"	Country Classic Cherry	7,740.
1520	43"	Queen Anne Oak	7,900.
1520	43"	Queen Anne Cherry	8,100.
1520	43"	Queen Anne Mahogany	8,100.
1500	45"	Ebony	7,320.
1500	45"	Polished Ebony	7,700.
1500	45"	Oak	7,000.
1500	45"	Walnut	7,260.
1500	45"	Mahogany	7,480.
1500	45"	Cherry	7,480.
1500	45"	Gothic Oak	7,440.

***For explanation of terms and prices, please see pages 20–25.**

Model	Size	Style and Finish	Price*

Walter, Charles R. (continued)

Grands

W-190	6' 4"	Ebony	32,200.
W-190	6' 4"	Semi-Polished and Polished Ebony	33,000.
W-190	6' 4"	Mahogany	33,600.
W-190	6' 4"	Semi-Polished and Polished Mahogany	34,400.
W-190	6' 4"	Walnut	33,600.
W-190	6' 4"	Open-Pore Walnut	32,800.
W-190	6' 4"	Semi-Polished and Polished Walnut	34,400.
W-190	6' 4"	Cherry	33,600.
W-190	6' 4"	Semi-Polished and Polished Cherry	34,400.
W-190	6' 4"	Oak	30,900.
W-190	6' 4"	Chippendale Mahogany	34,600.
W-190	6' 4"	Chip. Semi-Pol. and Pol. Mahogany	35,400.
W-190	6' 4"	Chippendale Cherry	34,600.
W-190	6' 4"	Chip. Semi-Pol. and Pol. Cherry	35,400.

Weber

Model numbers with two digits designate models from Korea, with three digits, from China.

Verticals

W-109	43"	Continental Polished Ebony	3,380.
W-109	43"	Continental Polished Walnut	3,500.
W-109	43"	Continental Polished Mahogany	3,500.
W-109	43"	Continental Polished White	3,440.
W-109	43"	Continental Polished Ivory	3,440.
W-41A	43"	Continental Polished Ebony	4,200.
W-41A	43"	Continental Polished Mahogany	4,460.
W-41A	43"	Continental Polished White	4,240.
WF-41	43"	French Provincial Cherry	4,800.
WF-108	43-1/2"	French Cherry	3,900.
WF-108	43-1/2"	Mahogany	3,900.
WF-108	43-1/2"	Italian Walnut	3,900.
WF-108	43-1/2"	Mediterranean Oak	3,900.
WF-108	43-1/2"	Queen Anne Cherry	3,900.

Model	Size	Style and Finish	Price*
WF-110	43-1/2"	French Cherry	4,300.
WF-110	43-1/2"	Mahogany	4,100.
WF-110	43-1/2"	Queen Anne Oak	4,300.
WFX-43	43-1/2"	French Cherry	5,200.
WFD-44	43-1/2"	Mahogany	5,500.
WFD-44	43-1/2"	Oak	5,500.
WFD-44	43-1/2"	French Provincial Cherry	5,600.
WSF-44	43-1/2"	French Cherry	6,790.
WSF-44	43-1/2"	Mediterranean Oak	6,790.
WSF-44	43-1/2"	Queen Anne Oak	6,790.
WSF-44	43-1/2"	Mahogany	6,790.
WS-46	46"	Ebony	4,990.
WS-46	46"	American Oak	5,180.
WS-46	46"	American Walnut	5,180.
WSE-48	47"	Polished Ebony	6,390.
WSE-48	47"	Polished Mahogany	6,590.
WSE-48	47"	Polished Brown Mahogany	6,590.
WSE-48	47"	Polished Walnut	6,590.
W-121	48"	Polished Ebony	4,460.
W-121	48"	Polished Mahogany	4,580.
W-121	48"	Polished Walnut	4,580.
WF-121	48"	Walnut	4,780.
W-48	48"	Ebony and Polished Ebony	5,800.
W-48	48"	Polished Mahogany	6,060.
W-48	48"	Polished Brown Mahogany	6,060.
W-131	52"	Polished Ebony	4,880.
Grands			
WG-150	4' 11-1/2"	Polished Ebony	9,500.
WG-150	4' 11-1/2"	Polished Mahogany	9,700.
WG-50	4' 11-1/2"	Ebony and Polished Ebony	11,980.
WG-50	4' 11-1/2"	Polished Walnut	12,860.
WG-50	4' 11-1/2"	Polished Mahogany	12,860.
WG-50	4' 11-1/2"	Polished Brown Mahogany	12,860.
WG-50	4' 11-1/2"	Cherry	13,260.
WG-50	4' 11-1/2"	Polished White	12,380.
WG-50	4' 11-1/2"	Polished Ivory	12,380.
WG-50	4' 11-1/2"	Queen Anne Polished Ebony	13,920.

***For explanation of terms and prices, please see pages 20–25.**

Model	Size	Style and Finish	Price*

Weber (continued)

WG-50	4' 11-1/2"	Queen Anne Polished Mahogany	14,900.
WG-50	4' 11-1/2"	Queen Anne Polished Brown Mahogany	14,900.
WG-50	4' 11-1/2"	Queen Anne Cherry	15,300.
WG-50	4' 11-1/2"	Queen Anne Oak	15,020.
WG-50	4' 11-1/2"	Queen Anne Polished Ivory	14,220.
WG-51	5' 1"	Ebony and Polished Ebony	13,000.
WG-51	5' 1"	Polished Walnut	13,720.
WG-51	5' 1"	Polished Mahogany	13,720.
WG-51	5' 1"	Polished Brown Mahogany	13,720.
WG-51	5' 1"	Cherry	14,120.
WSG-51	5' 1"	Polished Ebony	13,790.
WSG-51	5' 1"	Polished Mahogany	14,190.
WSG-51	5' 1"	Polished Brown Mahogany	14,190.
WSG-51	5' 1"	Empire Brown Mahogany	17,590.
WSG-51	5' 1"	Polished White	13,990.
WG-157	5' 2"	Polished Ebony	10,500.
WG-57	5' 7"	Ebony and Polished Ebony	15,120.
WG-57	5' 7"	Walnut and Polished Walnut	15,760.
WG-57	5' 7"	Polished Mahogany	15,760.
WG-57	5' 7"	Polished Brown Mahogany	15,760.
WG-57	5' 7"	Cherry	16,160.
WSG-57	5' 7"	Polished Ebony	15,790.
WSG-57	5' 7"	Polished Mahogany	16,390.
WSG-57	5' 7"	Polished Brown Mahogany	16,390.
WSG-57	5' 7"	Empire Brown Mahogany	19,390.
WSG-57	5' 7"	Polished Walnut	16,390.
WSG-57	5' 7"	Queen Anne Mahogany	18,790.
WSG-57	5' 7"	Queen Anne Cherry	18,990.
WG-175	5' 9"	Polished Ebony	11,300.
WG-60	6' 1"	Ebony and Polished Ebony	16,320.
WG-60	6' 1"	Polished Mahogany	16,660.
WG-60	6' 1"	Polished Walnut	16,660.
WSG-60	6' 1"	Polished Ebony	17,990.
WG-68	6' 10"	Ebony and Polished Ebony	21,200.
WG-70	7'	Ebony and Polished Ebony	26,300.
WG-90	9'	Ebony and Polished Ebony	62,090.

Model	Size	Style and Finish	Price*

Weinbach

Note: Prices below do not include bench. Add from $220 to $630 (most are under $400), depending on choice of bench.

Model	Size	Style and Finish	Price*
Verticals			
114-I	45"	Demi-Chippendale Polished Walnut	6,180.
114-I	45"	Demi-Chippendale Pol.Flame Mahog.	6,180.
114-IC	45"	Chippendale Polished Walnut	6,500.
114-IC	45"	Chippendale Polished Flame Mahogany	6,500.
114-II	45"	Polished Ebony	5,500.
114-II	45"	Polished Walnut	5,500.
114-II	45"	Polished Flame Mahogany	5,500.
114-IV	45"	Polished Ebony	5,900.
114-IV	45"	Polished Walnut	5,900.
114-IV	45"	Polished Flame Mahogany	5,900.
124-III	50"	Polished Ebony	7,100.
124-III	50"	Polished Walnut	7,100.
124-III	50"	Polished Flame Mahogany	7,100.
Grands			
155	5' 3"	Polished Ebony	18,780.
155	5' 3"	Polished Walnut	18,780.
155	5' 3"	Polished Flame Mahogany	18,780.
170	5' 8"	Polished Ebony	19,800.
170	5' 8"	Polished Walnut	19,800.
170	5' 8"	Polished Flame Mahogany	19,800.
170 C	5' 8"	Chippendale Polished Walnut	23,800.
170 C	5' 8"	Chippendale Polished Mahogany	23,800.
192	6' 4"	Polished Ebony	23,000.
192	6' 4"	Polished Walnut	23,000.
192	6' 4"	Polished Flame Mahogany	23,000.

***For explanation of terms and prices, please see pages 20–25.**

Model	Size	Style and Finish	Price*

Welmar

Prices are FOB England and do not include duty, freight, and other costs of importing. Oak, ash, and cherry are available at the same price as mahogany. Polished white is available at the same price as polished ebony.

Verticals

112	44"	Polished Ebony	10,770.
112	44"	Mahogany	9,270.
112	44"	Polished Mahogany	10,770.
112	44"	Walnut	9,270.
112	44"	Polished Walnut	10,770.
112	44"	Teak	9,270.
112 School	44"	Mahogany	9,840.
112 School	44"	Oak	9,840.
114	44"	Polished Ebony	11,010.
114	44"	Mahogany	9,675.
114	44"	Polished Mahogany	11,010.
114	44"	Walnut	9,675.
114	44"	Polished Walnut	11,010.
114	44"	Teak	9,675.
114 Regency	44"	Mahogany	10,320.
114 Regency	44"	Polished Mahogany	11,610.
118	46"	Polished Ebony	11,910.
118	46"	Mahogany	10,395.
118	46"	Polished Mahogany	11,910.
118	46"	Walnut	10,395.
118	46"	Polished Walnut	11,910.
122 School	48"	Mahogany	10,875.
122 School	48"	Oak	10,875.
126	50"	Polished Ebony	12,795.
126	50"	Mahogany	11,625.
126	50"	Polished Mahogany	12,795.
126	50"	Walnut	11,625.
126	50"	Polished Walnut	12,795.

Grands

186	6' 1"	Polished Ebony	37,785.

Westbrook (also Brentwood)

Model	Size	Style and Finish	Price*
Verticals			
CFR006	43"	Country French Cherry	2,938.
TR006	43"	Walnut	2,898.
TR006	43"	Oak	2,898.
MP005	43"	Polished Ebony	2,678.
MP005	43"	Polished Walnut	2,678.
MP005	43"	Polished Mahogany	2,678.
MP005	43"	Polished Cherry	2,678.
MP005	43"	Polished White	2,898.
MP012	48"	Polished Ebony	3,098.
MP012	48"	Polished Walnut	3,098.
MP012	48"	Polished Mahogany	3,098.
MP012	48"	Polished Cherry	3,098.

Wieler — see "Sängler & Söhne / Wieler"

Woodchester

Prices are FOB England and do not include duty, freight, and other costs of importing. Oak, ash, and cherry are available at the same price as mahogany. Polished white is available at the same price as polished ebony.

Model	Size	Style and Finish	Price*
Verticals			
Elmore	42"	Polished Ebony	5,640.
Elmore	42"	Mahogany	4,785.
Elmore	42"	Polished Mahogany	5,640.
Elmore	42"	Walnut	4,785.
Elmore	42"	Polished Walnut	5,640.
Elmore	42"	Teak	4,785.
Cantabile 'T'	44"	Polished Ebony	8,250.
Cantabile 'T'	44"	Mahogany	7,230.
Cantabile 'T'	44"	Polished Mahogany	8,250.
Cantabile 'T'	44"	Walnut	7,230.
Cantabile 'T'	44"	Polished Walnut	8,250.
Cantabile 'T'	44"	Teak	7,230.

Model	Size	Style and Finish	Price*

Woodchester (continued)

Arlingham	46"	Polished Ebony	6,075.
Arlingham	46"	Mahogany	5,250.
Arlingham	46"	Polished Mahogany	6,075.
Arlingham	46"	Walnut	5,250.
Arlingham	46"	Polished Walnut	6,075.
Arlingham	46"	Teak	5,250.
Burleigh	46"	Polished Ebony	9,375.
Burleigh	46"	Mahogany	8,220.
Burleigh	46"	Polished Mahogany	9,375.
Burleigh	46"	Walnut	8,220.
Burleigh	46"	Polished Walnut	9,375.
Burleigh	46"	Teak	8,220.
Cheltenham	46"	Polished Ebony	8,580.
Cheltenham	46"	Mahogany	7,695.
Cheltenham	46"	Polished Mahogany	8,580.
Cheltenham	46"	Walnut	7,695.
Cheltenham	46"	Polished Walnut	8,580.
Cheltenham	46"	Teak	7,695.
Kingscourt	46"	Polished Ebony	6,300.
Kingscourt	46"	Mahogany	5,385.
Kingscourt	46"	Polished Mahogany	6,300.
Kingscourt	46"	Walnut	5,385.
Kingscourt	46"	Polished Walnut	6,300.
Kingscourt	46"	Teak	5,385.
Concerto	48"	Polished Ebony	10,620.
Concerto	48"	Mahogany	9,435.
Concerto	48"	Polished Mahogany	10,620.
Concerto	48"	Walnut	9,435.
Concerto	48"	Polished Walnut	10,620.
Concerto	48"	Teak	9,435.
Gloucester	50"	Polished Ebony	7,890.
Gloucester	50"	Mahogany	6,765.
Gloucester	50"	Polished Mahogany	7,890.
Gloucester	50"	Walnut	6,765.
Gloucester	50"	Polished Walnut	7,890.
Gloucester	50"	Teak	6,765.

Model	Size	Style and Finish	Price*

Wurlitzer

Model	Size	Style and Finish	Price*
Verticals			
1175A	37"	American Country Regal Oak	3,530.
1176N	37"	Queen Anne Hallmark Cherry	3,530.
2270A	42"	Ribbon-Striped Mahogany	3,940.
2275B	42"	American Country Regal Oak	3,940.
2276B	42"	Queen Anne Hallmark Cherry	3,940.
WP50	42"	Continental Polished Ebony	2,700.
WP50	42"	Continental Polished Mahogany	2,700.
Grands			
C143	4' 7"	Ebony and Polished Ebony	10,030.
C143	4' 7"	Polished Mahogany	10,330.
C143	4' 7"	Polished Oak	10,330.
C143	4' 7"	Polished White	10,030.
C153	5' 1"	Ebony and Polished Ebony	11,600.
C153	5' 1"	Polished Mahogany	12,000.
C153	5' 1"	Walnut	12,000.
C153	5' 1"	Oak	12,000.
C153	5' 1"	Polished Ivory	11,600.
C153QA	5' 1"	Queen Anne Polished Mahogany	14,000.
C153QA	5' 1"	Queen Anne Oak	14,000.
C153QA	5' 1"	Queen Anne Cherry	14,000.
C173	5' 8"	Ebony and Polished Ebony	12,800.
C173	5' 8"	Polished Mahogany	13,190.
C173	5' 8"	Polished White	12,800.

Yamaha

Model	Size	Style and Finish	Price*
Verticals			
M112	44"	Continental Ebony	5,090.
M112	44"	Continental Polished Ebony	5,190.
M112	44"	Continental American Walnut	5,290.
M112	44"	Continental Polished Mahogany	6,390.
M112	44"	Continental Polished White	6,290.
M450	44"	American Oak	3,790.
M450	44"	Cherry	3,790.

***For explanation of terms and prices, please see pages 20–25.**

Model	Size	Style and Finish	Price*

Yamaha (continued)

Model	Size	Style and Finish	Price*
M500	44"	Cottage Cherry	4,890.
M500	44"	Country Manor Light Oak	6,390.
M500	44"	Country Villa White Oak	6,590.
M500	44"	Florentine Light Oak	4,890.
M500	44"	Georgian Mahogany	5,990.
M500	44"	Hancock Brown Cherry	4,290.
M500	44"	Milano Dark Oak	4,890.
M500	44"	Parisian Cherry	6,190.
M500	44"	Queen Anne Cherry	5,090.
M500	44"	Queen Anne Dark Cherry	5,090.
M500	44"	Sheraton Mahogany	4,290.
P22	45"	American Walnut	5,190.
P22	45"	Black Oak	5,190.
P22	45"	Dark Oak	5,190.
P22	45"	Light Oak	5,190.
T116	45"	Polished Ebony	5,390.
T116	45"	Polished Mahogany	6,390.
T121	48"	Polished Ebony	6,390.
U1	48"	Ebony	7,790.
U1	48"	Polished Ebony	7,990.
U1	48"	American Walnut	8,390.
U1	48"	Polished American Walnut	8,990.
U1	48"	Polished Mahogany	8,990.
U1	48"	Polished White	9,190.
U3	52"	Polished Ebony	10,690.
U3	52"	Polished Mahogany	11,990.
U5	52"	Polished Ebony	12,590.
U5	52"	Bubinga	21,990.
Disklavier Verticals			
MX500	44"	Country Manor Light Oak	11,190.
MX500	44"	Country Villa White Oak	11,390.
MX500	44"	Florentine Light Oak	9,790
MX500	44"	Georgian Mahogany	10,790.
MX500	44"	Milano Dark Oak	9,790
MX500	44"	Parisian Cherry	10,990.

Model	Size	Style and Finish	Price*
MX500	44"	Parisian Dark Cherry	10,990
MX500	44"	Queen Anne Cherry	9,990.
MX500	44"	Queen Anne Dark Cherry	9,990.
MX22	45"	American Walnut	10,190.
MX22	45"	Dark Oak	10,190.
MX22	45"	Black Oak	10,190.
MX22	45"	Light Oak	10,190.
MX116	45"	Polished Ebony	10,390.
MX116	45"	Polished Mahogany	11,390
MX1Z	48"	Polished Ebony	14,390.
MX1Z	48"	American Walnut	14,790.
MX1Z	48"	Polished Mahogany	15,390.
MX1Z	48"	Polished White	15,590.
MIDIPiano (Silent) Verticals			
MP500	44"	Cottage Cherry	7,590.
MP500	44"	Country Manor Light Oak	8,990.
MP500	44"	Country Villa White Oak	9,190.
MP500	44"	Florentine Light Oak	7,590.
MP500	44"	Georgian Mahogany	8,590.
MP500	44"	Hancock Brown Cherry	7,090.
MP500	44"	Milano Dark Oak	7,590.
MP500	44"	Parisian Cherry	8,790.
MP500	44"	Queen Anne Cherry	7,790.
MP500	44"	Queen Anne Dark Cherry	7,790.
MP500	44"	Sheraton Mahogany	7,090.
MP22	45"	American Walnut	7,790.
MP1Z	48"	Polished Ebony	10,590.
Disklavier Verticals with Silent Feature			
MPX1Z	48"	Polished Ebony	15,290.
MPX1Z	48"	American Walnut	15,690.
MPX1Z	48"	*Polished Mahogany*	16,290.
MPX1Z	48"	Polished White	16,490.

***For explanation of terms and prices, please see pages 20–25.**

Model	Size	Style and Finish	Price*

Yamaha (continued)

Grands

GA1E	4' 11"	Polished Ebony	9,990.
GA1	4' 11"	Polished Ebony	11,490.
GP1	5' 3"	Polished Ebony	13,390.
GH1B	5' 3"	Ebony	14,490.
GH1B	5' 3"	Polished Ebony	14,890.
GH1B	5' 3"	American Walnut	16,490.
GH1B	5' 3"	Polished American Walnut	16,490.
GH1B	5' 3"	Polished Mahogany	16,490.
GH1B	5' 3"	Polished Ivory	16,490.
GH1B	5' 3"	Polished White	16,090.
GH1FP	5' 3"	French Provincial Cherry	20,090.
GH1G	5' 3"	Georgian Mahogany	20,090.
C1	5' 3"	Ebony	18,690.
C1	5' 3"	Polished Ebony	19,090.
C1	5' 3"	American Walnut	21,390.
C1	5' 3"	Mahogany and Polished Mahogany	22,190.
C1	5' 3"	Polished White	21,390.
C2	5' 8"	Ebony	21,390.
C2	5' 8"	Polished Ebony	21,590.
C2	5' 8"	American Walnut	24,390.
C2	5' 8"	Polished American Walnut	25,190.
C2	5' 8"	Polished Mahogany	25,190.
C2	5' 8"	Light American Oak	24,390.
C2	5' 8"	Polished White	23,090.
C3	6' 1"	Ebony	29,090.
C3	6' 1"	Polished Ebony	29,290.
C3	6' 1"	American Walnut	32,090.
C3	6' 1"	Polished Mahogany	32,690.
C3	6' 1"	Neo	83,990.
C3	6' 1"	Bubinga	55,990.
C3	6' 1"	Bubinga Floral	57,990.
S4	6' 3"	Polished Ebony	52,490.
C5	6' 7"	Ebony	31,390.
C5	6' 7"	Polished Ebony	31,590.

Model	Size	Style and Finish	Price*
C6	6' 11"	Ebony	34,790.
C6	6' 11"	Polished Ebony	34,990.
S6	6' 11"	Polished Ebony	59,390.
C7	7' 6"	Ebony	39,690.
C7	7' 6"	Polished Ebony	40,090.
CFIIIS	9'	Polished Ebony	108,390.
Disklavier Grands			
DGA1	4' 11"	Polished Ebony (playback only)	19,990.
DGP1	5' 3"	Polished Ebony (playback only)	22,690.
DGH1BA	5' 3"	*Ebony*	28,130.
DGH1BA	5' 3"	Polished Ebony	28,530.
DGH1BA	5' 3"	American Walnut	30,130.
DGH1BA	5' 3"	*Polished American Walnut*	30,130.
DGH1BA	5' 3"	*Polished Mahogany*	30,130.
DGH1BA	5' 3"	*Polished Ivory*	30,130.
DGH1BA	5' 3"	Polished White	29,730.
DC1A	5' 3"	*Ebony*	32,330.
DC1A	5' 3"	Polished Ebony	32,730.
DC1A	5' 3"	American Walnut	35,030.
DC1A	5' 3"	*Polished American Walnut*	35,830.
DC1A	5' 3"	*Polished Mahogany*	35,830.
DC1A	5' 3"	*Polished Ivory*	35,830.
DC1A	5' 3"	*Polished White*	35,030.
DC2A	5' 8"	*Ebony*	35,030.
DC2A	5' 8"	Polished Ebony	35,230.
DC2A	5' 8"	American Walnut	38,030.
DC2A	5' 8"	*Polished American Walnut*	38,830.
DC2A	5' 8"	*Polished Mahogany*	38,830.
DC2A	5' 8"	Polished White	36,730.
DC3A	6' 1"	*Ebony*	43,330.
DC3A	6' 1"	Polished Ebony	43,530.
DC3A	6' 1"	American Walnut	46,330.
DC3A	6' 1"	*Polished Mahogany*	46,930.
DC3A	6' 1"	Polished White	45,530.
DC3A	6' 1"	"Neo" Aluminum and Cherry	98,230.
DC3A	6' 1"	Bubinga	70,230.
DC3A	6' 1"	Bubinga Floral	72,230.

***For explanation of terms and prices, please see pages 20–25.**

Model	Size	Style and Finish	Price*

Yamaha (continued)

DC5A	6' 7"	Ebony	45,630.
DC5A	6' 7"	Polished Ebony	45,830.
DC6A	6' 11"	Ebony	49,030.
DC6A	6' 11"	Polished Ebony	49,230.
DC7A	7' 6"	Ebony	53,930.
DC7A	7' 6"	Polished Ebony	54,330.
MIDIPiano (Silent) Grands			
MPC1	5' 3"	Polished Ebony	24,290.
MPC2	5' 8"	Polished Ebony	26,790.
MPC3	6' 1"	Polished Ebony	34,390.
MPC6	6' 11"	Polished Ebony	40,190.
MPC7	7' 6"	Polished Ebony	45,190.
Disklavier Pro Grands			
DC3APRO	6' 1"	Polished Ebony	51,490.
DS4APRO	6' 3"	Polished Ebony	76,890.
DC5APRO	6' 7"	Polished Ebony	53,790.
DC6APRO	6' 11"	Polished Ebony	57,190.
DS6APRO	6' 11"	Polished Ebony	83,790.
DC7APRO	7' 6"	Polished Ebony	64,090.
DC7Pro2000	7' 6"	Designer	297,990.
DCFIIISAPRO	9'	Polished Ebony	137,700.

Young Chang

See also under "Bergmann" and "Pramberger."

Verticals			
PE-102	43"	Continental Polished Ebony	3,390.
PE-102	43"	Continental Polished Red Mahogany	3,790.
PF-110	43-1/2"	Mahogany	4,700.
PF-110	43-1/2"	Mediterranean Oak	5,100.
PF-110	43-1/2"	French Provincial Cherry	5,500.
PF-110	43-1/2"	Queen Anne Cherry	5,300.
PF-110	43-1/2"	Queen Anne Oak	4,900.
PE-116	46-1/2"	Mediterranean Oak	5,790.
PE-116	46-1/2"	French Provincial Cherry	5,990.

Model	Size	Style and Finish	Price*
PE-116S	46-1/2"	Ebony	4,790.
PE-116S	46-1/2"	American Walnut	4,990.
PE-116S	46-1/2"	American Oak	4,990.
PE-118	47"	Ebony and Polished Ebony	4,700.
PE-118	47"	Polished Red Mahogany	4,990.
PE-118	47"	Polished Brown Mahogany	4,990.
PE-121	48"	Ebony and Polished Ebony	4,900.
PE-121	48"	Polished Red Mahogany	5,190.
PE-121	48"	Polished Brown Mahogany	5,190.
PE-131	52"	Polished Ebony	5,990.
Grands			
PG-150	4' 11-1/2"	Ebony and Polished Ebony	11,990.
PG-150	4' 11-1/2"	Polished Red Mahogany	12,590.
PG-150	4' 11-1/2"	Polished Brown Mahogany	12,590.
PG-150	4' 11-1/2"	Cherry	12,790.
PG-150	4' 11-1/2"	Polished Ivory	12,390.
PG-150	4' 11-1/2"	Polished White	12,390.
PG-150D	4' 11-1/2"	Queen Anne Polished Mahogany	14,790.
PG-150D	4' 11-1/2"	Queen Anne Cherry	14,990.
PG-150D	4' 11-1/2"	Queen Anne Polished Ivory	14,590.
PG-150KPS	4' 11-1/2"	Polished Ebony Kurzweil Player System	20,990.
PG-157	5' 2"	Ebony and Polished Ebony	13,500.
PG-157	5' 2"	Polished Red Mahogany	13,900.
PG-157	5' 2"	Polished Brown Mahogany	13,900.
PG-157	5' 2"	Cherry	14,100.
PG-157	5' 2"	Polished Ivory	13,700.
PG-157	5' 2"	Polished White	13,700.
PG-157D	5' 2"	Country French Cherry	16,790.
PG-157D	5' 2"	Queen Anne Mahogany	16,590.
PG-157D	5' 2"	Queen Anne Cherry	16,790.
PG-157D	5' 2"	Empire Polished Brown Mahogany	17,390.
PG-175	5' 9"	Ebony and Polished Ebony	15,390.
PG-175	5' 9"	Polished Red Mahogany	15,990.
PG-175	5' 9"	Polished Brown Mahogany	15,990.
PG-175	5' 9"	Walnut	15,990.
PG-175D	5' 9"	Empire Polished Brown Mahogany	19,390.

***For explanation of terms and prices, please see pages 20–25.**

Model	Size	Style and Finish	Price*

Young Chang (continued)

Model	Size	Style and Finish	Price*
PG-185	6' 1"	Ebony and Polished Ebony	17,590.
PG-185	6' 1"	Walnut and Polished Walnut	18,500.
PG-185	6' 1"	Polished Red Mahogany	18,500.
PG-185	6' 1"	Polished Brown Mahogany	18,500.
PG-185	6' 1"	Polished Ivory	18,300.
PG-208	6' 10"	Ebony and Polished Ebony	21,990.
PG-213	7'	Ebony and Polished Ebony	27,190.
G-275	9'	Polished Ebony	62,190.